A prescribed burn / Yoho National Park, British Columbia, Canada

EXTREME WILDFIRE

SMOKE JUMPERS, HIGH-TECH GEAR, SURVIVAL TACTICS, AND THE EXTRAORDINARY SCIENCE OF FIRE

MARK THIESSEN

WITH GLEN PHELAN

NATIONAL GEOGRAPHIC

WASHINGTON, D.C.

FOR MY MOTHER, WHO ENCOURAGED ME TO FOLLOW MY DREAMS.
—MARK THIESSEN

Since 1888, the National Geographic Society has funded more than 12,000 research, exploration, and preservation projects around the world. The Society receives funds from National Geographic Partners LLC, funded in part by your purchase. A portion of the proceeds from this book supports this vital work. To learn more, visit www.natgeo.com/info.

For more information, visit
www.nationalgeographic.com,
call 1-800-647-5463, or
write to the following address:
National Geographic Partners, LLC
1145 17th Street N.W.
Washington, D.C. 20036-4688 U.S.A.

Visit us online at nationalgeographic.com/books

For librarians and teachers: ngchildrensbooks.org

More for kids from National Geographic:
kids.nationalgeographic.com

For information about special discounts for bulk purchases, please contact National Geographic Books Special Sales: ngspecsales@ngs.org

For rights or permissions inquiries, please contact National Geographic Books Subsidiary Rights: ngbookrights@ngs.org

NATIONAL GEOGRAPHIC and Yellow Border Design are trademarks of the National Geographic Society, used under license.

Designed by James Hiscott, Jr.

Paperback ISBN: 978-1-4263-2530-4
Reinforced library binding ISBN: 978-1-4263-2531-1

Printed in China
16/PPS/1

❝ I'm supporting the Eric Marsh Foundation for Wildland Firefighters, and I think you should too. It's an all-volunteer organization where 100% of your donations go directly to aid the families of fallen wildland firefighters. Eric was one of the nineteen Granite Mountain Hotshots killed in the Yarnell Fire in 2013. Please support this foundation started by Eric's widow, Amanda. Please donate at: ericmarshfoundationforwildlandfirefighters.org.**❞**
—*Mark Thiessen*

A trailer is engulfed by flames in California, U.S.A.

CONTENTS

INTRODUCTION

I WAS IN IDAHO, U.S.A., photographing firefighters as they came away from the front lines of a raging wildfire. One by one, they made their way into camp for some much needed food and rest. They were all tired, sweaty, and dirty. Then up walked a firefighter with a chain saw slung over his shoulder. He was covered with soot and ash from head to toe. The cleanest spots on him were the whites of his eyes.

Those eyes were what caught my attention. They showed complete exhaustion, yet they also showed pride in his work and determination to complete it. To me, this firefighter is typical of the brave men and women who battle blazes in forests, grasslands, scrublands, and other wilderness areas. The pay isn't great, but they don't do it for the money. In fact, many wildland firefighters don't get paid at all. In the United States, nearly 80 percent of the first firefighters on the scene of a wildland fire are volunteers.

No matter how long on the job, paid or unpaid, these people see some of the most dramatic moments of their lives while fighting fires. I first witnessed such moments while covering wildfires as a newspaper photographer. It didn't take long for me to realize that fighting wildfires is more than a job—it's a remarkable way of life. I decided then that I wanted to examine this way of life up close.

I began my project by becoming certified as a wildland firefighter. This allowed me to share many of the firefighters' experiences so I could better understand what they go through. I then was able to use my camera to capture the drama of wildfires and tell the stories of the people who fight them. I share some of those incredible moments and stories with you in this book.

What's it like to be in a burning forest as roaring flames race from tree to tree? What goes through your mind as you are about to slide down a rope from a helicopter or parachute from a plane to fight a fire below? How does it feel to get doused by a load of cold, gooey fire retardant? Get ready to find out on the pages that follow.

That's not all. You'll learn the science behind wildfire—how it starts, how it spreads, and how it's stopped. You'll feel like you're battling the flames alongside the hotshots, smoke jumpers, and other wildland firefighters. During our adventures, you'll discover plenty of surprises, like how some plants and animals depend on wildfire to survive. We'll explore famous fires of the current and 20th centuries—some tragic—but all with important lessons to offer. You'll become "fire smart" as you learn how to prevent wildfires and how we can all live safely with this powerful force of nature.

I have photographed dozens and dozens of wildfires over the last 20 years. You might wonder why I constantly put myself in such risky situations. Safety is my top priority, as it is for all firefighters. Dangers are always present when fighting wildfires, but there are ways to keep track of and minimize the risks. Firefighters on the line accept these risks as they heroically do their jobs. I accept the risks for the privilege of telling their story. Usually no one is there with the firefighters to document what they do, to record the exciting moments as well as the quiet ones. I'm determined to change that with my lifelong photography project.

Mark Thiessen

This book is one of the results of that goal. I hope firefighters can show it to their loved ones and say proudly, "This is what I do."

Mark Thiessen

Seeley Lake / Montana U.S.A

CHAPTER 1
>>> The Science of Wildfire

[Wildfire—an uncontrolled fire in a forest, prairie, or other wilderness area]

A fire in Boise, Idaho, grows out of control in the shifting winds.

MY ESCAPE FROM A ROARING BLAZE

I WAS BUMMED.

MY TIME WITH THE FIRE CREW WAS NEARLY AT AN END, AND I HAD LITTLE TO SHOW FOR IT.

Many years ago I had spent nearly two weeks hanging out with wildland firefighters in Boise, Idaho. This city of more than 200,000 people is nestled at the bottom of forested hills and mountains. It's a beautiful part of the country, but I wasn't there to photograph the scenery—I was there to photograph fire. I wanted to document what it's like to battle a wilderness blaze. Through my photos, I wanted to show what wildland firefighters are up against. I wanted to tell their story.

But I seemed to pick the wrong weeks. There

Strong winds suddenly swept through the area. These winds fanned the dying flames and pushed them up the hill, where large shrubs quickly caught on fire. In a matter of minutes, the snaps and crackles became roars and rumbles as flames leaped from shrub to shrub and devoured the vegetation. The two-acre (0.8-ha) fire had grown to 15,000 acres (6,070 ha) by nightfall.

My senses were on full alert as I clicked off one dramatic photo after another. Danger was all around, but I wasn't terribly concerned about my safety or that of the firefighters working near me—until we heard on the radio that the wind was changing direction. We all stopped in our tracks. We looked up. The smoke that had been blowing away from us was now right above us. That meant the fire also was blowing our way.

Another shout came over the radio. "You guys gotta get out of there! And get that photographer out, too!" That photographer was me!

No one had to be told twice to leave. We ran toward a barbed-wire fence and hurried over it. The sharp barbs cut into our hands, but there was no time to nurse our wounds. Fire was hot on our heels. We raced across a field of dry grass and shrubs and reached a paved road. Less than a minute later, the field was ablaze.

It was a close call, but everyone escaped unharmed. The Eighth Street Fire, as it came to be known, was an experience I'll never forget.

were no fires. Then one afternoon near the end of the trip, things changed. You might say they heated up.

I was pumping gas into my car, when I noticed a wisp of smoke rising from the distant foothills. I drove back to the fire station near the airport. As I entered the parking lot, I saw all the firefighters run outside and look toward the foothills. Then they sprinted for their gear, jumped into their trucks, and sped off toward the smoke. I followed close behind.

By the time we reached the fire, it was almost out. A line of small flames no higher than my waist was burning its way through the dry, tan grass near the base of a hill. The fiery line stretched the length of a couple football fields. The flames quietly snapped and crackled, like the crunching of plastic wrap in your hands. Several crews were already on the scene, and they seemed to have the fire under control. Soon, all that remained was a 20-foot (6-m) line of flames by the hill. "That's good," I thought. But I still wondered if I'd ever experience a big blaze.

Then the weather changed.

Notes From the Field

THANKS TO THE EFFORTS OF FIREFIGHTERS, the Eighth Street Fire damaged only one house. But it destroyed the habitat of more than 250 kinds of animals. Reptiles, birds, and mammals lost the places where they lived and found food. Twenty years later, however, many animals have moved back into the area. Some birds still have not returned because the trees in which they nest haven't yet grown tall enough.

A RECIPE FOR FIRE

BEING IN THE MIDDLE OF A WILDFIRE SHOWED ME HOW DANGEROUS A FORCE IT CAN BE.

The smoke and flames can kill. Fire can damage and destroy houses as well as wildlife habitat. In addition, it can strip away the vegetation that holds everything in place, increasing erosion, or the wearing away of soil and bits of rock. Rain can easily wash these loose materials down bare hillsides and into streams, where the eroded soil can pollute and clog community water supplies.

In spite of the harm it causes, I am fascinated with wildfire. I want to further understand this extreme force of nature. You, too, can understand it. To begin, all you have to do is picture a birthday cupcake.

A small candle on the cupcake flickers with a bright, yellow flame. Now imagine setting a large glass jar upside down over the cupcake. What happens to the flame? Within seconds, it gets smaller and smaller until it goes out completely. Why? Because the burning candle used up one of the ingredients needed for fire—oxygen.

The air around us is a mixture of gases. About 21 percent of that mixture is oxygen. We need oxygen to breathe, and fire needs it to burn. Most buildings have plenty of oxygen to keep a flame going. Plus, more air—and oxygen—

seeps in from outside all the time through vents and cracks. But the upside-down jar sealed in only a small amount of air. The burning candle used up the oxygen until there wasn't enough to keep the flame going. So the flame went out.

Oxygen is one of three ingredients in the recipe for fire. The other two are heat and fuel.

Where did the heat come from to light the birthday candle? The source of heat was probably a flame from a match or a lighter. Okay, so what was the source of heat for *those* flames? That answer is friction, which is the force of two surfaces rubbing against each other. Friction produces heat. You can feel this heat when you rub your hands together quickly. Heat from the force of friction ignites a match when it's rubbed against a rough surface. In a lighter, metal parts rub against each other to make a spark that lights a flame.

The last ingredient of fire is fuel. Any material that burns is fuel. Guess what the fuel is for the birthday candle. Did you say the candle wick? That seems to make sense, since the fabric wick is the part that's lit. But things aren't always as they seem. In reality, the fuel is the candle wax! Here's how it works. The flame's heat melts wax at the top of the candle. The liquid wax is then drawn up the wick, like milk being sucked up a straw. On the wick, the flame heats the liquid wax enough to turn it into a gas. The gas mixes rapidly with oxygen and burns, keeping the flame going until it's blown out.

Fire retardant reduces oxygen and heat.

HEAT, FUEL, AND OXYGEN are needed to create fire. These three ingredients make up the three sides of the fire triangle. Looking at this model makes it easier to understand fire. If you remove any one of the sides of a triangle, the triangle cannot exist. If you remove any one of the ingredients of a fire, the fire cannot exist.

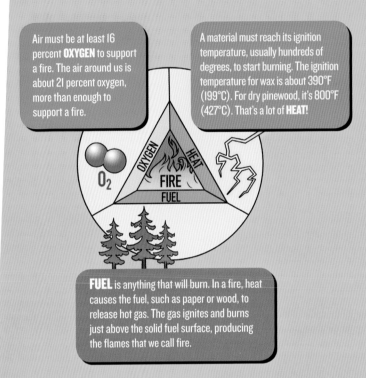

Air must be at least 16 percent **OXYGEN** to support a fire. The air around us is about 21 percent oxygen, more than enough to support a fire.

A material must reach its ignition temperature, usually hundreds of degrees, to start burning. The ignition temperature for wax is about 390°F (199°C). For dry pinewood, it's 800°F (427°C). That's a lot of **HEAT!**

FUEL is anything that will burn. In a fire, heat causes the fuel, such as paper or wood, to release hot gas. The gas ignites and burns just above the solid fuel surface, producing the flames that we call fire.

>>> EXTINGUISH A CANDLE FLAME

To extinguish any fire, you have to take away at least one side of the fire triangle. Here are three ways to do that for a lighted candle.

1. **TAKE AWAY OXYGEN.**
   Cut off the oxygen supply by covering the candle. You saw this with the glass jar. The burning candle quickly uses up the limited oxygen and goes out.

2. **TAKE AWAY HEAT.**
   When you blow out a candle, you take away heat. The moving air cools the flame enough to make it go out.

3. **TAKE AWAY FUEL.**
   You can use heat-resistant gloves or tongs to squash the wick. This prevents the wax from moving up the wick and feeding the fire. The flame goes out.

Now you know how the fire triangle applies to candles. But how does it work for wildfires?

Flames race across dry brush in Ventura County, California.

A RECIPE FOR WILDFIRE

FIREsmarts

BE SMART ABOUT CAMPFIRES. Never leave a campfire unattended. Before leaving a campsite or going to bed, have an adult help you completely douse the fire with water and stir the ashes until they are cold. Then you can be sure that no hot pieces of wood remain that might flare up later.

DURING THE EIGHTH STREET FIRE,

we knew we had to sprint across a field of dry grass and shrubs. Vegetation is fuel for a wildfire. And the drier the vegetation, the faster it burns. So the field we ran through was prime fuel, with the fire right behind us.

Once a wildfire starts, it gobbles up any fuel it can find—from majestic trees to rotting stumps to scraggly broken roots sticking out of the ground. Dead leaves, twigs, and pine needles on the forest floor burn quickly. Even underground roots and other vegetation just below the surface heat up enough to ignite. Wooden cabins and other structures are fuel, too.

So a wildland fire has a lot of fuel to keep it going. And, of course, the air in the great outdoors provides plenty of oxygen. But what about the "heat" side of the fire triangle? Where does the heat come from to make that first bit of fuel burst into flame? The answers may surprise you.

Most of the initial heat comes from people. In fact, people start about nine out of ten wildfires. Here are a few ways that carelessness leads to the fiery destruction of field and forest.

- 🔥 Someone discards a match or cigarette that isn't completely put out.
- 🔥 Campers leave a campfire smoldering. Then a breeze scatters hot bits of wood to nearby fuels.
- 🔥 Cinders from exploded fireworks remain red hot as they drift to the ground.
- 🔥 Someone starts a small fire to burn yard waste. Then the fire gets out of hand when a wind comes up.
- 🔥 A discarded piece of glass focuses enough sunlight to heat up and ignite a clump of dry grass.

When wildfires start naturally, lightning is usually the culprit. Although lightning is part of a thunderstorm, rain from the storm is often too brief to douse, or put out, the flames. In fact, sometimes the rain evaporates in the dry air before ever reaching the ground.

Lightning is a giant spark of electricity, but other kinds of sparks will start a fire, too. Imagine a rock tumbling down a cliff. The rock slams against other rocks. Friction from the collisions breaks off tiny specks of hot glowing rock—sparks—and sends them flying into some dry brush. Sometimes that's all it takes. No wonder more than 75,000 wildfires occur in the United States each year!

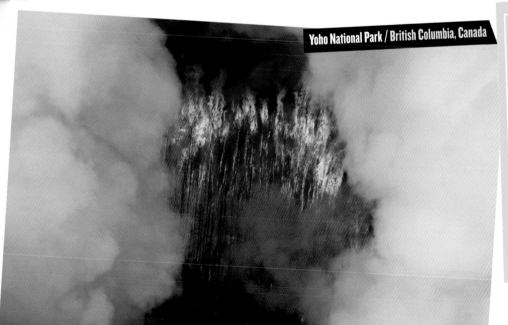

Yoho National Park / British Columbia, Canada

NATURE'S SIGNAL

SMOKE—If you notice a wildfire in the distance, chances are you see the smoke before you see the flames. Smoke is a sure sign that something is burning. Wildfire smoke is a mixture of gases, tiny liquid droplets, and fine solid particles called soot that don't burn up during the fire. The rising heat from an intense fire lifts smoke high into the air. Then it moves with the winds.

15

FIZZLING
FLAMES OR
MONSTER
BLAZE?

The roots of a toppled tree burn in California.

FIREfact

WILDFIRES GIVE OFF RED-HOT EMBERS. These pieces of fuel burn enough to glow but not enough to produce flame. Often an ember bursts into flame if more oxygen reaches it. That's why people rearrange logs in a campfire or fireplace. Lifting logs on top lets oxygen reach the embers hidden beneath, and a fire that looked burned out then comes roaring back to life.

TWO FIRES
START IN THE
WILDERNESS.

One grows no larger than a swimming pool, and firefighters put it out in a couple of hours. The other fire barrels across the countryside, scorching tens of thousands of acres. It takes several weeks before firefighters are able to stop it. Why does one fire fizzle out quickly and another fire grow into a monster blaze? It largely depends on the fuel, the shape of the land, and the weather.

>>> FUEL

The size and arrangement of fuel can help keep a fire small or give it a boost. Fuel burns faster if it's in smaller pieces. You probably know this if you have helped light a campfire. You don't start by holding a match to the logs. You first light small twigs beneath the logs. The twigs are kindling that catch fire easily and burn with enough heat to start the logs on fire.

In a wildfire, smaller vegetation like dead leaves, pine needles, dry grass, and broken twigs can act as kindling for larger fuels such as fallen logs and stumps. Flames can spread upward from these ground fuels to the tops of trees, but the flames usually need "bridges" or "ladders." Hanging branches, saplings, and large bushes are the ideal ladder fuels to carry flames to the treetops, or crown, of a forested area.

The kind of fuel matters, too. For example, pine trees burn faster and hotter than hardwoods such as oak, because pine has more resin. This thick, gooey liquid is very flammable. One of the most flammable fuels is the shrubs and brushlands that make up areas in California and the American Southwest. The fine branches of the plants found in these areas burn easily during dry conditions.

>>> TOPOGRAPHY

The shape of the land, or topography, also affects how wildfire spreads. If a fire is near the bottom of a hill, chances are it will soon be at the top. To understand how, imagine a group of sports fans passing a ball up a set of crowded bleachers. The people on the bottom hand the ball to the people behind them. Those people hand the ball to the people behind *them.* Up and up the ball goes, until it's at the top of the bleachers.

Now replace the bleachers with a forested hillside. Trees at the bottom are aflame, and the rising heat from the fire heats up and dries out the trees directly above it on the hillside. Flames from the tops of trees below reach the lower branches of trees above. These higher trees catch fire easily because they have been dried out from the rising heat. The heat and flames move from one level of trees to the next, quickly reaching the hilltop.

>>> WEATHER

Weather plays a major role in how a wildfire spreads. Hot, dry, and windy conditions are a wildfire's friends. Cool, wet, and calm conditions are its enemies.

Hot, dry weather draws moisture out of plants, so they ignite more easily. This is one reason wildfires tend to start and spread most during the afternoon, when the weather is hottest and driest. On the other hand, cool and wet conditions slow a fire. So a raging fire tends to slow down and cool down at night, when the air temperature drops.

Day or night, wind is a wildfire's very best friend. The stronger the wind blows, the faster the fire goes. But wait a minute. You might be thinking, if you can blow out a candle, shouldn't a strong gust of wind be able to blow out a wildfire? Not usually. The heat from a typical wildfire is too great to be cooled and extinguished by even the strongest winds. Instead, the wind helps dry out the fuel and can send the front of a fire racing across the landscape.

If that weren't enough, winds toss flaming pieces of fuel and hot, glowing embers into unburned areas. Spot fires pop up everywhere. Wind may be fire's best friend—but it's a firefighter's worst enemy.

"WE'RE CUT OFF!"

ON A HOT, DRY EVENING IN EARLY JULY 2007,

lightning struck in a canyon near Hot Springs, South Dakota, U.S.A. The flames immediately began working their way down the length of the canyon and up the forested slopes. Fire officials helped evacuate people from houses located near the rim of the canyon. Their goal was to save as many of these homes as possible.

One house was built up against a grove of trees. Firefighters realized the fire was growing quickly and getting hotter and hotter. They knew that if such an intense fire reached those trees, it would reach the house. So their plan was to fight fire with fire. They would start fires to burn the trees and other vegetation close to the house. This controlled burn would create a safety zone by using up the fuel before the main fire could get to it.

They had already burned off an area around the house, but they needed to take out more trees in back. One young firefighter began this important task. His supervisor left his truck in the safety zone and walked toward the young firefighter to check on the controlled burn. The supervisor was going to be out of the truck for only a few minutes, so he didn't take his radio or his gloves. He also left his fire shelter, a foldable structure that helps protect a trapped firefighter.

Conditions were changing rapidly. Winds picked up. One gust nearly tore an opened truck door off its hinges. Spot fires from embers were popping up all over the place, and they were growing. Part of the main fire had come out of the canyon and was

Hot Springs
South Dakota
Cut Off Firefighters

Lightning, like this bolt over the plains of South Dakota, starts many wildfires.

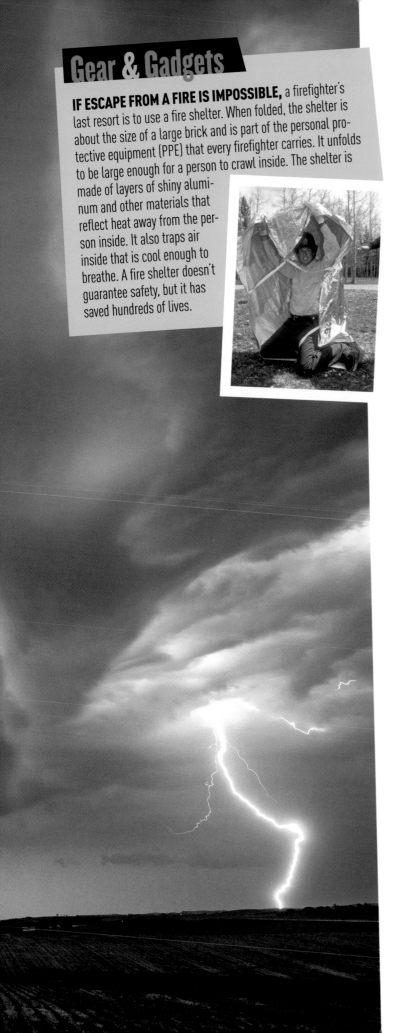

Gear & Gadgets

IF ESCAPE FROM A FIRE IS IMPOSSIBLE, a firefighter's last resort is to use a fire shelter. When folded, the shelter is about the size of a large brick and is part of the personal protective equipment (PPE) that every firefighter carries. It unfolds to be large enough for a person to crawl inside. The shelter is made of layers of shiny aluminum and other materials that reflect heat away from the person inside. It also traps air inside that is cool enough to breathe. A fire shelter doesn't guarantee safety, but it has saved hundreds of lives.

heading across a meadow toward the firefighters. Other parts of the canyon glowed orange and red as the blaze climbed toward the rim. Flames from spot fires met up with fire from the controlled burn among the trees. This cut off the two firefighters from the safety zone around the house.

The two firefighters turned in all directions. Walls of flame surrounded them. The supervisor grabbed the young firefighter's radio. "We've been cut off," he notified the operations chief. "We've got to make a run for it!"

Their goal now was to survive, and there were no good options. The supervisor scanned the landscape. The flames coming at them through the meadow were only two feet (0.6 m) high. Their best chance was to jump over the flames into the burned area beyond. They ran toward the fire, but before they could reach it, conditions changed again. A blast of hot wind fanned the flames, which suddenly grew to be as tall as a three-story building. No way could they survive that kind of heat.

Now the best option lay in a wall of six-foot (1.8-m) flames of an expanding spot fire. They sprinted toward it. At the last second, they raised their arms to cover their faces and jumped through the flames.

The firefighters came through the wall of flames unharmed, but they were far from safe. Smoke made it tough to breathe. They could barely see. Flaming trees pelted them with sizzling embers. Worst of all, blasts of heat from those burning trees were unbearable. That's when the young firefighter deployed his shelter.

They had only the one shelter, so they both crawled inside it. The shelter protected them from some of the heat, but they didn't stay in it for long. The young firefighter was having more difficulty breathing. The supervisor acted immediately, crawling out to radio for help. Finally, they got a break. Two fire engines appeared in the distance through the smoke and flames. The firefighters ran toward the engines while carrying the shelter as a heat shield. A few moments later, they reached their rescuers.

Now, finally, they were safe.

ACCOUNTS OF FIRES, LIKE THE ONE YOU JUST READ, ARE MORE THAN EXCITING STORIES.

They are important learning tools. Firefighters review videos and personal accounts of fires. Then they discuss what happened. How did the fire change? What was predictable, and what wasn't? What went right and what went wrong when fighting the fire? Lessons learned from these reviews help firefighters do their job better and improve safety. These lessons are especially important for people training to be firefighters. That's why fire reviews are an essential part of fire school.

Anyone who wants to be a wildland firefighter goes to fire school. This training program lasts only five days, but those days are packed with information and action. Here's a taste of what I experienced in fire school.

Each day begins with exercise. After all, you have to be physically fit to fight fire in the rugged wilderness. It takes strength, endurance, and flexibility to spend hours at a time cutting down trees, digging out stumps, ripping out shrubs, and chopping up roots to remove fuel. And it takes a special kind of person to do this amid the flames and smoke of a raging fire.

A workout of stretching, sit-ups, pull-ups, and other exercise is topped off with a little run or hike—of maybe three to five miles (5 to 8 km). This kind of endurance training helps prepare trainees for a pack test later in the week. Each trainee has to complete a three-mile (5-km) hike in 45 minutes while carrying a pack weighing 45 pounds (20.4 kg).

Besides physical ability and mental toughness, firefighters need knowledge about fire. So a major part of each day is spent learning what fire is, how it burns, how it moves, and how it behaves. For example, did you know fire produces its own winds?

Firefighters practice digging line.

FIRE SCHOOL

Notes From the Field

DURING OUR PRACTICE FIRE, a few people dug line so fiercely that they forgot about technique, or the correct way to do it. They dug, chopped, and scraped the grass harder and faster than anyone else. But they couldn't keep up that pace. In addition, they were trying to do all the work with their upper body muscles instead of using their leg muscles. They were worn out in 20 minutes.

Firefighters put out a fire at a simulation training facility.

As hot air rises from a fire, cooler air rushes in to take its place. That rush of air is wind. Firefighters use this knowledge to know where to set controlled burns so that the flames will be pulled in toward the main fire and not toward a structure or area they are trying to protect.

Trainees at fire school also learn how to use firefighting equipment, such as the pumps on fire engines. They learn proper techniques for handling tools, like a Pulaski. The head of this tool has an ax on one side, for cutting and chopping, and a hoe on the other side, for digging and scraping.

The most important lessons in fire school are how to stay safe. Fighting fires is risky, there's no doubt about it. But fire school teaches ways to reduce these risks. For example, one handy guideline is, "Keep one

TOP: Firefighters must remain in excellent shape to battle wildfires.

BOTTOM: Firefighters learn how to carefully set and control prescribed burns.

foot in the black, and you'll always come back." Can you figure out what this means? In a fire, the "black" is any burned out area. The "green" is any area that hasn't burned yet, whether it's actually green, tan, or some other color. If firefighters stay near the black, they can always get to it if they need to escape from the fire. Since the black area has already burned, it likely won't burn again, so it's a safety zone.

After several days of school, it's time to put the training to work. The trainees are grouped into crews. Then a practice fire is lit, and the crews have to put it out. Most of the crewmembers fight the small grass fire by digging line. This means using Pulaskis and other tools to clear a path of any vegetation along the front of the fire. This path is usually about three feet (1 m) wide and is called a fire line, or firebreak.

Digging line is the main way to control and put out a wildfire. It is exhausting, backbreaking work. Firefighters might dig line 14 hours a day on a real fire. The practice fire usually is out after one or two hours. It's a tough two hours when you're not used to it, but you get a terrific sense of accomplishment.

FIREfact

WHEN I COMPLETED FIRE SCHOOL, I received an Incident Qualification Card, also called a Red Card. This card is helpful when I'm photographing fires because it tells firefighters that I know how to stay safe. They know I won't get in their way taking photographs while they're trying to do their jobs. Each year I take a refresher course to sharpen my skills and knowledge and keep up my Red Card status. All wildland firefighters continue training throughout the fire season—from late spring to early fall. They review and discuss videos of fires, go over safety guidelines, and keep up a daily physical fitness program.

THE BIG BLOWUP OF 1910

Results of the Big Blowup in Idaho

ON AUGUST 20 AND 21, 1910, FIRES RAGED

across much of northern Idaho and northwestern Montana, U.S.A. The fires started in different places and in different ways. Some were caused by lightning, some by campfires, and still others by sparks from braking trains. It had been a dry spring and summer, so there was plenty of fuel ready for burning. Once the flames started, winds of near hurricane strength spread the blazes quickly.

Firefighters tried heroically to contain the fires, but success came only when the winds subsided and rain and snow fell the following days. The fires, collectively called the Big Blowup or the Big Burn, scorched more than three million acres (1,214,057 ha). The smoke reached Boston, nearly 2,200 miles (3,541 km) away. Tragically, 85 people died, including 78 firefighters.

One group of about 40 firefighters was lucky. They were trapped by the towering flames, when a forest ranger named Ed Pulaski led them to safety in a mineshaft. Does that name sound familiar? Ed Pulaski invented the Pulaski tool.

The Big Blowup had a lasting impact on how people fight fires. Before 1910, wildfires were sometimes left to burn, especially smaller ones. Some people were in favor of this because it reduced the amount of fuel on the ground, which helped prevent large disastrous fires. Other people thought every fire should be put out, no matter how small.

After the Big Blowup, the debate was over. Leaders of the U.S. Forest Service, which manages national forests in the United States, were determined to never let such a tragic fire happen again. So they decided they would fight every fire.

This policy lasted until about 1970. Then the Forest Service began to realize that sometimes the best way to prevent large fires really was to let little ones burn. They understood that fire could be helpful as well as harmful, as you'll discover in chapter 4.

HOW TO TRAIN LIKE A WILDLAND FIREFIGHTER

WILDLAND FIREFIGHTERS train every day to stay physically fit. So can you. Start by making a weekly Activity Plan. Make a chart for the week, leaving lots of room to write in activities for each day.

Use the Activity Chart to fill out your weekly Activity Plan. List a combination of activities that you can do. You might exercise that much already. Terrific! Keep it up! Maybe add a new activity now and then. Plan a mix of activities, so that you include at least one exercise that is rated Fair, Good, or Excellent for building strength, endurance, and flexibility. And remember, the Activity Chart shows only a small sampling of activities. There are lots of ways to exercise and stay fit.

>>> ACTIVITY PLAN

SUNDAY	MONDAY	TUESDAY	WEDNESDAY	THURSDAY	FRIDAY	SATURDAY

>>> ACTIVITY CHART

ACTIVITY	STRENGTH	ENDURANCE	FLEXIBILITY
Basketball	Poor	Good	Poor
Bicycling	Fair	Good	Poor
Calisthenics (e.g., push-ups, sit-ups, jumping jacks)	Good	Excellent	Excellent
Canoeing	Poor	Fair	Poor
Dancing	Fair	Good	Excellent
Gymnastics	Excellent	Excellent	Excellent
Hiking	Good	Excellent	Fair
Jumping Rope	Poor	Good	Poor
Skating (inline)	Poor	Excellent	Poor
Swimming	Fair	Good	Fair
Tennis	Poor	Fair	Poor
Volleyball	Fair	Poor	Poor

Division supervisor Fred Sanford evacuates his firefighters from Seeley Lake, Montana.

CHAPTER 2

>>> Battling Wildfire From the Ground

X

[Hotshots—Highly trained crews who use hand tools to fight on the front lines of wildfire; Engine crews—Firefighters who use vehicles and water to fight wildfires]

Capturing a BLIZZARD of Embers

AS I GOT OFF THE FREEWAY, I COULD SEE THE LONG, ORANGE GLOW

of fire in the hills above Santa Clarita. This part of California, about an hour's drive from downtown Los Angeles, is no stranger to wildfire. Nearly every year, at least one big fire chews through large patches of the grasses and shrubs that carpet the slopes surrounding the Santa Clarita Valley. The fires often are driven by the Santa Ana winds. These strong, dry winds blow through the mountain passes of Southern California toward the coast.

The Santa Ana winds were fierce that night, pushing the fire and carrying a long stream of smoke off into the night sky. I followed the glow as I drove through a neighborhood and into a sparsely populated area. Police had blocked off an intersection, but I showed them my media pass and they waved me through.

Soon I came upon an area where all the streetlights were out. It was totally dark except for the fire glow just beyond a slight incline. When I reached the top, I could barely believe my eyes. Countless orange and red sparks flew across the sky at tremendous speed. The strong winds blowing across a field that had burned were now whipping up a blizzard of embers.

I quickly pulled over, grabbed my camera attached to its tripod, and ran across the street. I climbed over a fence and into the field. Wind gusts bombarded me with embers and ash. The hot,

Warm Lake / Idaho

In Santa Clarita, California, each ember can spawn an entirely new fire.

Notes From the Field

FIREFIGHTERS TALK ABOUT BEING "BIT BY THE FIRE BUG." Once they experience their first wildfire season, most are drawn back year after year. What's the attraction? The desire to protect lives and property certainly plays a major role. But for many, it's also the challenge and thrill of facing down a powerful fire. They love the excitement and adventure of it. I, too, have been bitten by the fire bug, but in a different way. I'm drawn both by the desire to help and by the spectacular visual moments that wildfire provides—like an ember blizzard.

glowing bits stung my neck and ears like pinpricks. But I was more concerned about my eyes. What a time to be without goggles! I had been in such a rush to get to the fire from the airport that I'd forgotten them somewhere deep inside my suitcase.

However, I did have a substitute for goggles—my camera! I looked through the lens to protect my eyes and shielded my face with my hands as best I could. I didn't dare pull away from the camera and risk getting hot embers in my eyes.

The view through the lens was incredible. The scene was so otherworldly, so surreal. I took some half-second exposures to capture this amazing blizzard of sparks. Each delicate ember left its orange trail on the camera's sensor.

I was thankful to be in the right place at the right time. The photos show a beautiful side of one of nature's most extreme forces.

FIRE LOOKOUTS

WHEN A FIRE STARTS
IN A CITY OR TOWN, FIREFIGHTERS USUALLY LEARN OF IT QUICKLY.
The smoke might set off an alarm, or someone will see the fire and call 9-1-1. Within minutes, firefighters can be on the scene to rescue victims, put out the flames, and save property.

It can be a lot different with wildfires. Suppose embers from a forgotten smoldering campfire drift into a patch of dry pine needles. Fifteen minutes later, a ponderosa pine is going up in smoke, with flames spreading to other trees. Hikers a couple miles away cannot see the smoke through the forest and are unaware of the danger. No one else is around to let firefighters know a fire is burning. So how do they find out? Fortunately, fire lookouts are on duty.

A fire lookout watches the landscape from a building or tower on a mountaintop in search of wildfires. The views are spectacular. From the glass-walled perch, a lookout can see thousands of square miles of wilderness. Somewhere in that vast expanse, a new fire may be sending up its first wisps of smoke. It's the lookout's job to spot it. Powerful binoculars help.

Once the fire is spotted, the lookout peers through the sights of an instrument called a fire finder to get the location of the fire. Then he or she calls in the information to the fire dispatcher, who relays it to fire crews.

The job doesn't end there. The lookout continues to monitor and report the fire's progress. He or she helps to keep track of fire crew movements and positions. Lookouts also monitor weather conditions and report on wind shifts based in part on how the smoke is drifting. All of this information helps firefighters decide how best to attack the fire.

Many countries around the world use fire lookouts, including the United States, Canada, Mexico, Brazil, Australia, New Zealand, Russia, Israel, and several European countries. Some lookouts are stationed near urban areas, such as on the summit of Mount Tamalpais overlooking San Francisco, U.S.A. Here, the lookout can drive up to the tower each day. But most towers are in remote areas far from cities, towns, or even roads. The lookout lives in the tower or in a nearby cabin throughout the fire season.

Scott Mountain Lookout / Idaho

These can be lonely months. The occasional hikers who stop by are welcome company, but most days are quiet. Time passes slowly ... watching ... waiting .... Then a storm rolls in, and things get exciting fast. Clouds build. Lightning flashes. Gray curtains of rain drift across the horizon. The lookout not only has a front row seat to this spectacular show but also may be right in the storm's path.

Being in a lookout tower in the middle of a thunderstorm is intense. As the storm unleashes its electrical energy, the blinding flashes of lightning are constant, like strobe lights. The sudden booms of thunder make even a seasoned lookout shiver. Electrical charges build up on the lookout's body, making hair on the arms stand up and tingle. The air literally buzzes. The lookout is safe because a system of steel rods and cables draws electricity away from the building and into the ground. But being surrounded by a storm while perched on a mountaintop is still a wild ride.

Even before the storm clears, the lookout must keep a sharp eye on the terrain. Such an onslaught of lightning tends to produce multiple fires. Some of them may smolder at the base of a tree or bush for days. They might die out on their own. Or they might flare up a couple weeks later. When they do, they won't escape the watchful eyes of the lookout.

FIREfact

IN THE YEARS AFTER THE BIG BLOWUP, about 8,000 lookout towers were built across the United States. After 1960, much of this early wildfire detection system was abandoned in favor of aircraft and satellites. Yet a lookout is often the best way to spot a wildfire early, and about 300 towers are still used for that purpose. Other towers have become scenic viewing spots for visitors. Want to get a taste of life as a lookout? The U.S. Forest Service rents out many towers for overnight stays.

31

A high school baseball field is used as a fire camp in Hayfork, California.

FIRST
on the
SCENE

ON A WARM, BLUE-SKY AFTERNOON,

a fire lookout peers through a pair of binoculars at a distant, rising wisp of smoke. She speaks into her radio.

"Dispatch, this is Alpine Meadow Lookout. I have a smoke report."

"Go ahead, Alpine Meadow."

"I have a smoke sighted at one-five-three degrees."

"Copy that, Alpine Meadow, 153 degrees. And how far from the tower?"

"I estimate five miles away."

"Okay, Alpine Meadow, we'll get a chopper in the air to check it out. Dispatch clear."

Fifteen minutes later, the lookout hears the helicopter pilot over the radio.

"Dispatch, this is Bravo-220. We're over the smoke now. It's about halfway up the east slope of Bear Mountain. I'd put its size at about two acres."

"Copy that, Bravo-220. Keep an eye on it. I'll contact the Incident Commander."

Ten minutes pass.

"Dispatch, Bravo-220. The fire is moving upslope fast. It's about 50 acres now."

Every five to ten minutes, Bravo-220 radios an update to Dispatch, and every five to ten minutes the fire has nearly doubled in size. After a half hour, it shows no signs of slowing down. Fire crews are already on their way.

This example, while not from an actual lookout or fire, shows how firefighting professionals might respond to the initial sighting of a smoke. Among the first people on the scene is the Incident Commander, or IC. The IC is the main person in charge. He or she decides how best to fight the fire. If the fire is small and moves slowly, it may require only a few firefighters to put it out. But if it spreads quickly and grows into a major fire, hundreds or even thousands of firefighters and other professionals may be involved for weeks or months. Such a major fire requires a fire camp.

A fire camp often resembles a town made out of tents and trailers. In fact, it really is a mini town of sorts. It can be set up overnight to provide everything needed to battle a blaze. Here, firefighters can get some much-needed rest between shifts, along with food, water, and medical treatment. One tent might have satellite phones and laptops with Internet connection so firefighters can stay in touch with family and friends. Other tents hold all sorts of supplies, from bandages and batteries to hoses and chain saws. There are trailers for sophisticated mapping equipment and trailers for showers. Large fire camps even have stores.

Fire camp also is the headquarters for the Incident Commander and other supervisors who make the major decisions about fighting the fire. Another section of fire camp is the media center. Here, news reporters can find out the latest information about the fire and inform the public.

Notes From the Field

A FIRE CAMP MIGHT BE CONSTRUCTED on a school grounds, in a park, or in a field—any open area close enough to quickly get people and supplies to the fire but far enough away to be safe. Occasionally, the fire gets too close to the camp. Then everyone has to "bug out." They break camp and set up in a safer area within 24 hours.

eXpert Tips

FIGHTING WILDFIRES No matter how big or how small a wildfire is, fighting it requires three basic steps.

1. SIZE UP THE FIRE. The Incident Commander sizes up the fire (the "incident") by gathering all the information about it. Where is it? How big is it? How is it moving? What's the topography like? What fuels are involved? What's the weather forecast?

2. DEVELOP A PLAN. After sizing up the fire, the IC and other members of the management team develop an Incident Action Plan. What kinds of crews are needed? How many? Where do they dig line? Where are the escape routes and safety zones? Which risks are worth taking and which are not? There's a lot to decide.

3. IMPLEMENT THE PLAN AND REASSESS. Now the IC puts the plan into action. All the while, he or she is in contact with crew leaders and other supervisors. The management team keeps track of the firefighters' progress and how well the plan is working. If the fire changes strength or direction, other plans are in place to reduce risk for those on the front lines.

WHEN FIRE JUMPS THE ROAD

THE BURNOUT OPERATION IN MONTANA HAD BEEN PLANNED FOR DAYS.

The idea was to purposely burn out all the trees and brush between the dirt road that we were on and the fire's flaming flank high up on the ridge. This would leave nothing else for the fire to burn, and the firefighters and I would have good black right down to the road.

The plan called for an aerial ignition. In aerial ignition, a helicopter is filled with thousands of small balls that look like table tennis balls. Each ball contains a powdered substance. Just before the balls are dropped, they are injected with automobile anti-freeze. A chemical reaction between the two substances causes the balls to catch fire a few minutes after they hit the ground. This method is used when a large area needs to be burned out in a safe way.

From a truck on the opposite ridge, I watched the helicopter fly back and forth across the mountain-side. Soon, small wafts of smoke began to sift through the treetops into the clear sky, signaling that the balls had ignited. Down below, fire crews began to set fire to the vegetation along the road. As expected, this roadside fire was being drawn up into the larger aerial ignition fire by that fire's rising heat.

As the burnout continued, I rode with the Division Supervisor on patrol. We drove past crews setting fires on one side of the road, while other crews stood guard on the green side of the road to watch for spots. All it takes is one ember to drop into the green, and the fire has jumped the road. No one wanted that.

Suddenly, things didn't feel right. The bright sun-light dimmed. The clear blue sky became an eerie orange as smoke blocked the sun. The wind had shifted. Instead of the smoke column drifting up the burning mountainside, it was bending back over the road and drifting over the green side. We knew what that meant. Soon, embers that were pulled up into the smoke column would drop out on the other side of the road and start spot fires. And that's exactly what happened.

The supervisor's radio crackled with word that the fire had jumped the road in several places behind us. Crews ran into the forest with hoses hooked up to water trucks to extinguish the small fires, but more kept popping up.

We jumped out of the supervisor's pickup and went into the forest to investigate. The bright orange of spot fires glowed deep into the green. Then trees next to the road on the burnout side began torching—quickly going up in flames with a loud WHOOSH! As they did, they threw massive amounts of heat, smoke, and embers over our heads. Danger was increasing by the second.

The supervisor had a radio in each hand, listening to his crews and giving orders. As hard as they tried, they couldn't keep up with the spots. The supervisor decided it was time to order his crews to evacuate to the safety zone. He and I were the farthest into the forest and had to get out as well. We ran to the pickup, hopped inside, rolled up the windows, and took off.

All we could see was a wall of dark smoke ahead and fire on each side. We couldn't tell what was beyond the smoke, but we had to drive through it anyway. The flames were right up against the road, and they sort of guided us out.

Everyone met up in our safety zone. The supervisor made sure each crewmember was accounted for. All we could do at this point was sit back and watch the fire burn around the meadow the rest of the afternoon. The burnout ended up being a lot bigger than planned, but at least everyone was safe.

Notes From the Field

THE BURNOUT FROM THIS AERIAL IGNITION took place during the Jocko Lakes Fire of 2007 in northwestern Montana. A lookout first spotted the fire on July 18, but fire crews and aircraft were unable to locate it. Perhaps the fire died down quickly. It must have remained smoldering, however, possibly in a rotting log, because two weeks later, it flared up. This time, everyone could see it! Huge flames raced through the woodlands. Residents evacuated the nearby town of Seeley Lake. The town was spared, but the fire scorched more than 36,000 acres (14,569 ha) of forest.

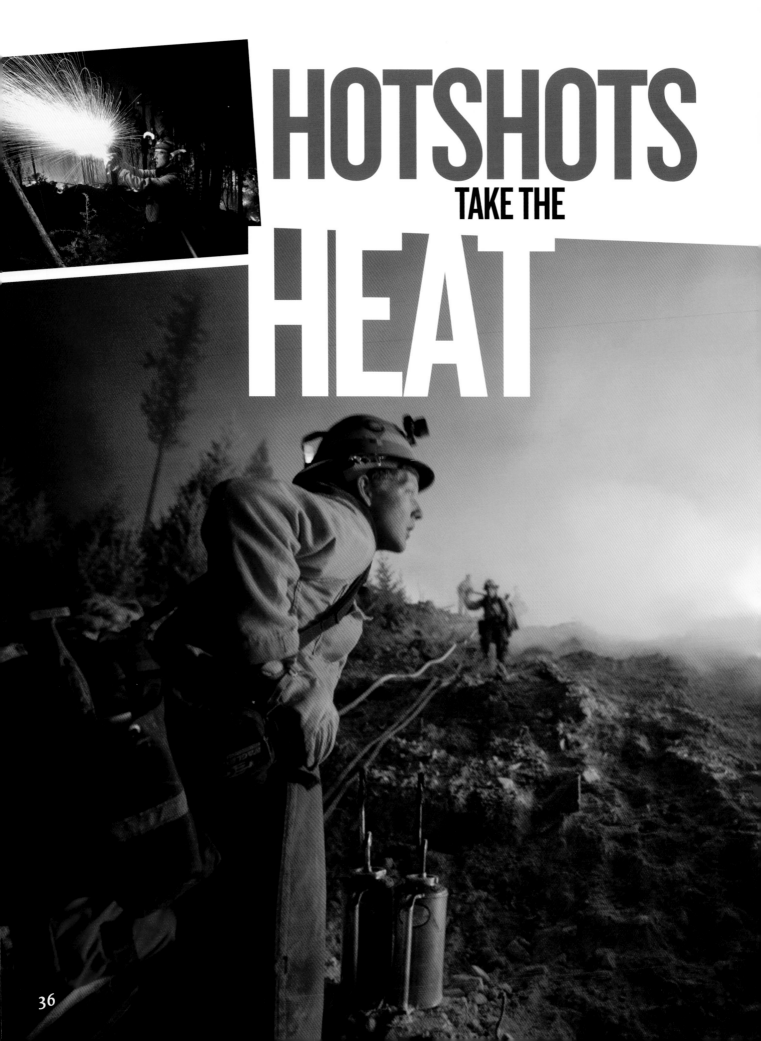

HOTSHOTS
TAKE THE
HEAT

IT TAKES SEVERAL KINDS OF FIREFIGHTERS TO EXTINGUISH A WILDFIRE.

Perhaps the most elite crews are the hotshots. The name says it all. Hotshots often are in the hottest, most dangerous part of the fire, closest to the flames. If a fire is tough to reach and looks difficult to put out, the hotshots go in. They're not reckless daredevils, though. Hotshots are highly trained and in tip-top physical condition. They know fire—how it acts, how to fight it, and how to stay safe from it—better than anyone.

Hotshots usually work in the most remote areas, far from roads. For this reason, they may have to hike for miles over steep, rugged terrain just to get to the fire. If time is critical, helicopters might fly them in. They take only what they can carry—food, water, safety gear, chain saws, and hand tools.

When hotshots reach a fire, they may be there for a while. Often too far from fire camp to go back and forth each day, they work and live in the wilderness for days in a row. Where do they sleep? On the softest patch of ground they can find—a safe distance from the flames, of course!

A hotshot crew consists of twenty firefighters, though they typically break up into two squads of ten. Then they can work on different parts of the fire at the same time. Also, one squad can work while the other one rests. This way they can battle the blaze during the night when the cooler temperatures and higher humidity make the fire easier to control. Day or night, one crewmember always stands lookout to warn others if the fire suddenly changes strength or direction.

Working only with the tools they carry, hotshots control the fire's advance by digging fire line. It's like saying, "Okay, Fire. We'll let you burn up to here, but that's it. You can't go any farther."

TOP: A flare is used to start a burnout fire in Seeley Lake, Montana.

Firefighters in Seeley Lake, Montana, take advantage of night's lower temperatures and humidity.

FIREfact

ABOUT 2,200 HOTSHOTS work for the U.S. Forest Service, Bureau of Land Management, National Park Service, and Bureau of Indian Affairs. That means about 110 hotshot crews are available in the United States. This may sound like a lot, but during a busy fire season, these crews get spread dangerously thin. One fire may require a couple dozen hotshot crews. They travel from fire to fire all over the country and sometimes to Mexico and Canada. It's no wonder these men and women are so highly respected in the firefighting community.

A firefighter burns out vegetation in Idaho.

PARTS OF A WILDFIRE

EVERY WILDFIRE SPREADS OUTWARD from where it starts, mostly driven in the direction of the wind. As it moves, it develops a pattern with recognizable parts.

>>> POINT OF ORIGIN
This is where the fire starts. It spreads outward from here.

>>> PERIMETER
This is the edge of the fire. The perimeter changes as the fire moves.

>>> HEAD
The fire spreads fastest at its head and shows the direction the fire is moving. The head usually has the tallest flames.

>>> HEEL
The heel is at the part of the fire that is opposite the head. Flames burn low, and the fire spreads slowly because it is moving against the wind or downslope.

>>> FLANKS
This is the part of the perimeter parallel to the direction of the fire. Think of the flanks as the sides of the fire.

>>> FINGERS
The topography or a localized wind gust might cause narrow extensions, or fingers, to grow from the fire's main body.

>>> SPOTS
Embers start spot fires outside the main fire's perimeter.

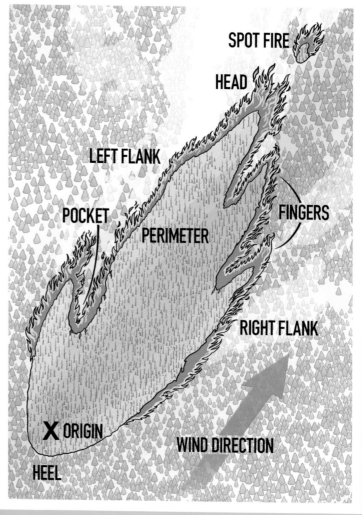

SPOT FIRE
HEAD
LEFT FLANK
POCKET
PERIMETER
FINGERS
RIGHT FLANK
X ORIGIN
WIND DIRECTION
HEEL

Hotshots excel at digging line. Their swings are precise, and they know how to dig without tiring too quickly. Their first swings break up the soil and chop out roots. Then they scrape at the ground until there's nothing that can burn. The axe blades of their Pulaskis easily chop through saplings. But what about the large trees? No problem. Step aside for the sawyers! These hotshots are the chain saw operators. All it takes is one angled cut to make a tree lean the right way, then one straight cut to bring it down.

Firefighters usually start digging line at the heel of the fire and work their way along the flanks toward the head. If the flames are low and just creeping, the crew can dig right next to them. The line they dig will likely stop that part of the fire in its tracks. If the flames are tall and moving quickly, it's too dangerous to dig close to them. So the line is constructed away from the fire's edge. Then crewmembers set fires to burn out the fuel between the line and the main fire.

What happens when things go wrong? The hotshots, like all fire crews, have already planned their escape routes and safety zones. Most escape routes are the fire lines themselves, but they also could be roads or creeks. Escape routes lead to safety zones, such as a burned-out area, a hillside of rocks, or a meadow away from the fire.

Gear & Gadgets

A PROPERLY EQUIPPED wildland firefighter wears and carries this gear:
- Flame-resistant clothing, like the yellow shirts and green pants of U.S. Forest Service firefighters
- Boots of high quality, usually leather; soles should be stitched on, not glued—the glue melts in the heat of a fire!
- Hard hat
- Leather gloves
- Safety goggles
- Gas mask
- Fire shelter
- Canteens of water
- Fusees (small flares used to start burn-out fires)

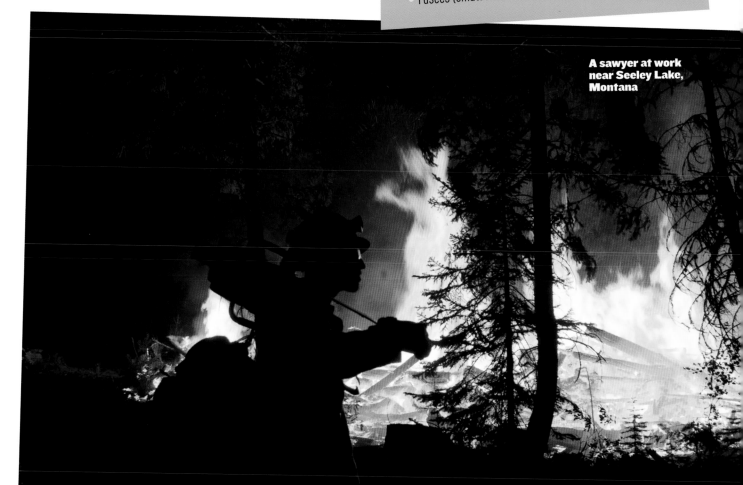

A sawyer at work near Seeley Lake, Montana

ENGINES
AND DOZERS

An engine crew evaluates the fire from a safe distance in Seeley Lake, Montana.

IF A WILDFIRE IS CLOSE TO ROADS

or in relatively flat terrain, engine crews lead the attack. Teams of three to ten firefighters use fire engines to get water on the flames. These are not the big red trucks you see in cities and towns. Those vehicles couldn't stand up to the rugged pounding from bumpy dirt roads and open wilderness.

Instead, wildfire engines are heavy-duty off-road vehicles. They can turn off a paved road and rumble across a range of sagebrush to get to a fire. On board are hand tools, chain saws, water pumps, hundreds of feet of hose, and up to 800 gallons (3,028 L) of water. While water is not the main weapon against wildfire, it is still useful. It extinguishes smaller fires. And for bigger ones, water cools and slows down the flames, giving firefighters more time to dig line.

Some engine crews "pump and roll," or "fog and jog." Two engines, one behind the other, roll slowly along the edge of a fire. Crewmembers jog alongside spraying the fire with a mist of water pumped from the engines. This one-two punch conserves water and usually puts out the flames of a low fire in dry areas.

What happens when the water tanks run dry? There are no hydrants out in the wilderness, but there may be streams or lakes. Pumps draw water from these sources through the hoses to replenish the tanks. Some vehicles are used just to carry water to portable containers set up near a fire. These containers, called "pumpkins," provide another 800 gallons (3,028 L) of water and may be filled many times during the fire. Sometimes firefighters pump water directly from streams or lakes onto the flames. Then thousands of feet of hose might be seen snaking its way over the ground.

Besides water, engines can spray fire retardant foam. This is used mostly on houses and other buildings. The foam helps prevent a building from igniting by cooling the fuel and blocking oxygen from reaching it.

Not all heavy firefighting vehicles have wheels and tanks. Some have tracks and blades. These are bulldozers. Most firefighters just call them dozers. The powerful machines are a tremendous help in digging line. A dozer's huge front blade not only plows up hardened ground with ease, it also can dig up stubborn stumps. If the cab is enclosed, dozer drivers can dig line right up against large flames radiating heat at 2,000°F (1,093°C) for a few minutes at a time.

A fire tornado / Yorba Linda, California

NATURE'S SIGNAL

FIRE WHIRLS—One of the most amazing and memorable sights in a wildfire is a fire whirl. This is a spinning column of hot rising air that carries smoke and flame high up into the sky. It's sometimes called a fire tornado. It's not a real tornado, but it can look as frightening as one. A fire whirl often indicates that extremely hot rising air is colliding with turbulent winds. These winds are forced to change direction suddenly as they meet an obstacle like a rock formation. The sudden change in direction makes the winds twist as they are pulled upward into the column of rising air. Flames are pulled up with the rising air as well. Hot rising gases from the burning vegetation may suddenly ignite as they meet fresh oxygen, adding to the whirling flames.

Cold trailing

MOP-UP

FIRE LINE HAS BEEN DUG AROUND THE **PERIMETER OF THE MAIN FIRE** AS WELL AS THE SPOT FIRES. It looks like all the flames are out. So now the weary firefighters can go home, right? Not even close. Now comes the most grueling and, in some ways, the most dangerous part of firefighting—mop-up.

Mop-up consists of putting out every smoking patch of ground, no matter how small, within 100 feet (31 m) inside the perimeter of the fire line. Firefighters walk through the burned-out areas—the black—and smother any smokes with shovelfuls of dirt.

Smoldering tree stumps are a huge problem for mop-up. Fire can work its way through a tree's root system, smolder all winter long, and then flare up in unburned areas in the spring. So firefighters can't just smother the stump with dirt. It has to come out, along with its major roots.

Mop-up is dangerous work, even though there are no flames or searing heat. In fact, many firefighter deaths and injuries occur during this stage of a fire.

The danger comes mostly from snags. These are trees that were dead before the fire and can fall easily. When fire burns around the base of a snag, the base might smolder after the fire is out. This gradual, flameless burning eats away at the base of the trunk. The base can weaken so much that the tree falls without warning. Mop-up includes cutting and removing snags so that they don't present a hazard in the months and years ahead.

Other dangers occur when crews mop up on a hillside or at the bottom of it. Tree roots that may have held boulders in place might be burned out or weakened. The rocks are now loosened and can come crashing down. Fallen logs on slopes are dangerous, too. Imagine a heavy log rolling or sliding down a hillside, loosening other logs and taking out snags. You wouldn't want to be in the way. To make the situation safer, firefighters dig trenches to hold the logs in place.

So after all the stamping, digging, prying, cutting, pulling, and trenching, there's one crucial mop-up task left. It's called cold trailing. Twenty firefighters stand five feet (1.5 m) apart in a line from the perimeter to a hundred feet (31 m) into the black. They walk slowly in this line, sweeping through the entire perimeter. As they walk along, they bend down and feel the ground with their bare hands. If anyone finds a hot spot, the entire line stops until the hot spot is dug up and cooled.

Is cold trailing really necessary? You bet it is. Remember that small practice fire I helped put out in fire school? We cold trailed it four times, and new smokes were still popping up. Mop-up on a typical fire can last a couple months. It's tedious, dirty, backbreaking, and risky work. When it's finally done, you can be sure the fire crews look forward to a few days of rest ... before heading off to the next fire.

A firefighter mops up the perimeter of a spot fire in Hayfork, California.

43

BLACK SATURDAY BUSHFIRES

FEBRUARY 7, 2009, BEGAN LIKE MOST OTHER SATURDAYS IN THE AUSTRALIAN STATE OF VICTORIA.

People were looking forward to a fun and relaxing weekend. But although the day dawned sunny and clear, much of the skies would soon be clouded in thick, billowing, gray smoke. Throughout Australia, this day would be known as Black Saturday.

Fire and government officials had warned people that weather conditions were setting up perfectly for wildfires. It was the middle of summer in the Southern Hemisphere, and for several days the temperature had been well above 100°F (38°C). On that Saturday, the temperature in Melbourne, the state's capital city, reached a record 115°F (46°C). The air was bone-dry, too. The average humidity in Melbourne is about 52 percent. That day, it was 6 percent. To top it off, winds were kicking up at 62 miles an hour (100 km/h). These extreme weather conditions provided the perfect storm for wildfires.

From mid-morning until early evening, nearly 400 wildfires burned through the scrublands and woodlands of this southeastern section of Australia. They started in various ways. Lightning sparked some. Others were spot fires from embers. Some fires were the result of arson, which is the crime of purposely setting a fire to cause harm or damage. Many fires began when high winds knocked over power lines.

The fires were fierce and devastating. Flames reached more than 300 feet (91 m) into the air. Smoke clouds rose nine miles (15 km) high. Some towns lost nearly every home. In all, 173 people died, and more than 400 were injured. Many of the blazes continued through February and into early March. Then, thankfully, cooler temperatures and rains swept the region. This welcome change in the weather helped firefighters contain and extinguish the remaining fires.

The bushfires of Black Saturday show that some fires are simply too big for firefighters to extinguish, at least without a helping hand from nature. The bushfires also are a reminder of what wildland firefighters may face when they respond to those first wisps of smoke spotted in the distance.

The aftermath of Black Saturday in Yarra Valley, Victoria, Australia

HOW TO LOCATE A DISTANT OBJECT

LOCATING A FIRE can be tricky, even for experienced lookouts. So fire managers often get readings from two lookouts.

Each lookout sees the smoke from a different position. A line from each lookout to the smoke is drawn on a map. The fire is located where the lines intersect, or cross.

You can use this same general method to locate a distant object, like a tower. Choose an object that is at least a couple miles (3 km) away. Try to view the object from high points, such as the upper floor of a building or a hill. Then follow these steps:

1. Find a map of the area in which your object is located. The map should have an arrow pointing north and include a scale that shows units of distance. Make sure it is a map that you can draw on.

2. Go to one location to view your distant object. Mark this location on the map as A.

3. Align the map so that the north arrow is facing north in your location.

4. Look out at the landscape to find your distant object.

5. Looking at your distant object, mark where you think it exists on your map. Use distinct objects and landmarks to help estimate its location. Then draw a line on the map from your location through the location you marked for your distant object.

6. Go to your second location so that you can view your object from another angle. Mark the location on the map as B.

7. Repeat steps 3–5.

8. The place where your two lines intersect should be the location of your distant object. Use the map scale to figure out how far away the object is.

9. If you can, go to the distant object. Use your map to help you find it. How accurately did you locate it? Would you say you were spot on? Fairly close? If you were way off, don't get discouraged. Even real lookouts have to practice their skills to get accurate readings.

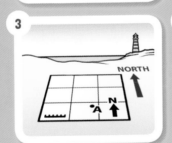

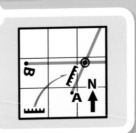

An air tanker douses a wildfire near Provence, France.

CHAPTER 5

>>> # Battling Wildfire From the Air

[Helitack—The use of helicopters to attack a wildfire by transporting firefighters and equipment, and by dropping water or fire retardant; Smoke jumper—A wildland firefighter who reaches a fire by aircraft and parachutes or rope]

How to Drop Out of the SKY

Packed into an Mi-8 helicopter, a weary crew returns to base in Siberia, Russia.

WAS I REALLY GOING TO JUMP OUT OF A PERFECTLY GOOD AIRCRAFT? I had to prepare to shoot photos for a story about Russian smoke jumpers. These daring firefighters get to a wildfire fast by either parachuting out of an airplane or rappelling out of a helicopter. To accompany these smoke jumpers, I would have to get to the fires the way they do. There wasn't time to learn how to parachute, so I would have to learn how to rappel.

I trained at the Rapattack Base in British Columbia, Canada. Things started slowly. After learning how to use the equipment, my first rappel was from only 10 feet (3 m). But then the rappels got higher—40 feet (12 m), 50 feet (15 m), and, finally, 60 feet (18 m)—all from inside an enclosed tower.

Notes From the Field

I WAS STANDING IN LINE with Russian smoke jumpers ready to exit the helicopter. I heard several loud bangs behind me. The person setting up our rappel gear—the loadmaster—was pulling the descenders out of their bag and dropping them on the metal floor. BANG! CLANG! I cringed, remembering how I was taught to handle those devices with the greatest care. Yet the banging didn't seem to bother anyone else, so I shrugged it off. One by one the smoke jumpers stepped out and descended. Then it was my turn, but my exit was a little different. The loadmaster attached my descender to the rope, made sure I'd gotten all my equipment in order, then grabbed me by the harness and lifted me out the door! Slightly stunned, I began my rappel. Not exactly the way I was trained, but the result was the same—a safe trip to the ground.

Standing on a platform in the tower, I wore a harness wrapped over my shoulder, around my waist, and between my legs. Attached to the harness was my rappel device, called a descender. The rope slides through this hunk of metal shaped like a figure 8. I was taught that the descender was the single most important piece of equipment, because my life depended on it. The instructors told me to cradle it like a baby when I climbed back up the stairs. If I

dropped it or banged it on a railing, I was to tell them. They would take it out of service and have it tested for cracks.

The first time I stepped off a platform, I admit I was a bit nervous. Dangling in midair, my eyes followed the rope up to the steel beam to which it was attached. Then I eased the rope through the descender and slid right down to the ground. Piece of cake! I made about 30 rappels from higher and higher platforms. I soon

A Russian smoke jumper jumps from an AN-2 plane.

Notes From the Field

HERE'S SOMETHING I NEVER EXPECTED. Sometimes the rope thickens during a rappel. It happens because of the "rotor wash," as the twirling rotors push the air down and compress it. This means the gases in the air directly beneath the rotors get pressed together, including molecules of water vapor. The concentration of water molecules increases, which makes the air more humid. It's like the force of the rotors is squeezing water out of the air. If the humidity gets high enough, the rope absorbs enough water to swell notice-ably. During training, sometimes the rope got so thick it didn't slip smoothly through the holes of the descender. I had to force the rope through, which was tough to do with my weight pulling on it.

discovered that rappelling was exhilarating, but climbing all those stairs was exhausting!

The following day, it was time to rappel from a helicopter. I climbed aboard, and up we went. We hovered a few hundred feet above a meadow. Speaking is useless over the roar of the engines, so my instructor used prearranged hand signals to guide me through each step of the process.

I sat next to the open door and thought, "Here goes nothing!" Following the instructor's signals, I attached the rope to my descender, unlatched my seat belt, and climbed out onto the runner of the helicopter.

I was immediately met by a downward blast of air from the whirling rotors above. I'd been warned about this "rotor wash," but I didn't fully understand until I experienced it. The sound vibrated through my entire body with each WHUP of the rotor blades.

I leaned back and eased some rope through the descender until my waist was even with the run-ner—one of the "skis" that the helicopter lands on. Then I let out more line and pulled my feet off the runner. Now I was suspended hundreds of feet above the meadow. Like the previous day, I looked up at the metal arm holding the rope. Except this time that metal beam was connected to a hovering helicopter, not to the ground. What a strange feeling. It seemed impossible that such a heavy machine could just hang in the air like that. And here I was looking up at the bottom of it! Weird.

But I wasn't here to contemplate the physics of flight. As I had rehearsed in the tower, I eased the rope through the descender and dropped like a spider on a silk thread. In just a few seconds, my feet touched the ground, and I disconnected from the rope. After several more rappels from the copter, I felt ready for my adventure in Russia.

THE MOST IMPORTANT

and effective resources for putting out wildfires are the firefighters on the ground. But often this ground attack needs some help from the air. Air attack provides speed, access, information, and other resources that help put out the flames.

If firefighters can get to a small fire quickly, chances are they can put it out before it grows into a raging inferno. That's the idea behind helicopter attack, or helitack. A helicopter gets a crew to the fire fast, usually before anyone else. Helitack is especially useful if a fire is in a remote, rugged area. The helicopter might land if there's a safe place to do so. Otherwise, crewmembers rappel to the ground. Then they unload equipment and supplies lowered from the helicopter.

Once on the ground, the helitack crew hustles to dig line around the fire and set backfires if necessary. The firefighters might also clear a landing zone for the helicopter. That makes it easier to bring in more crews and supplies if needed. After all, why rappel if you can just land and hop out? A landing zone also provides a place where the helicopter can pick up the firefighters when the job is done. That might not be for a day or two, even for a small fire.

Helicopters are used in other ways to fight wildfires. They sometimes transport hotshots and smoke jumpers. They carry supplies from fire camp to the front lines. Helicopters also can hover and maneuver in ways that other aircraft can't. That makes them valuable as "eyes in the sky." Helitack crews can pinpoint the location of fires, report their movement, and check the progress of firefighting efforts.

Another very important job of helitack is to perform water drops. This means dousing the fire with water from a bucket that hangs beneath the helicopter. Where do the pilots get the water? Anywhere they can find it! They might dip into lakes, ponds, streams, or even swimming pools.

Gear & Gadgets

THE BRIGHT RED BUCKETS that helicopters carry for water drops are officially called helibuckets or monsoon buckets, but most U.S. firefighters call them Bambi Buckets. Different-size buckets hold anywhere from 72 to 2,600 gallons (273 to 9,842 L) of water. From inside the helicopter, a crewmember can open the bottom of the bucket to fill it up as well as to release the water. Some buckets can also deliver fire retardant foam.

A helibucket in action

SMOKE JUMPERS

A smoke jumper trains over Montana.

WHAT DO YOU GET WHEN YOU COMBINE SKYDIVING WITH FIREFIGHTING? YOU GET SMOKE JUMPING!

Sometimes smoke jumpers catch a ride on a helicopter. Usually, however, they get to fires by parachuting from an airplane. It sure makes for a dramatic entrance, but they don't do it for the drama. Planes and parachutes may simply be the fastest way to get firefighters to the scene. This is especially true in the most remote of areas, such as the vast forests that carpet mountainous regions in the United States, Canada, and Russia.

Smoke jumpers focus on small fires. In many cases only a single tree is aflame, usually from a lightning strike. Then, like a helitack crew, the smoke jumpers quickly dig line to corral the fire and keep it from growing. If the fire does spread and become more than the smoke jumpers can handle, hotshots join the battle.

Smoke jumper crews vary in size depending on the size of the fire. When the call comes in, as few as two or as many as twenty smoke jumpers will suit up, load the plane, and take off. If there are multiple small fires in an area, several crews of three or four might parachute to the different locations from the same plane.

Notes From the Field

SMOKE JUMPERS ARE FOLLOWED OUT THE DOOR by parachute drops of supplies and equipment. This cargo includes hand tools, chain saws, gasoline, and drip torches in case backfires need to be started. The firefighters may be there for a couple days, so they also need enough food, water, and medical supplies. They have their parachutes and jumpsuits, too. What do they do with all this stuff when their work is done?

If they're lucky, a helicopter picks up the crew and cargo. If copters are unable to land in the rugged terrain, sure-footed mules might be brought in to carry out the cargo as the smoke jumpers hike alongside to a pickup point. Sometimes, the smoke jumpers have to carry out their own cargo.

Training / Idaho

I-2-3 JUMP!

THE PLANE APPROACHES THE FIRE'S LOCATION. Twelve or so smoke jumpers are ready to go. But they don't just pile out and take their chances. Here's the 3-step procedure to make sure they hit their mark safely:

1. FIND A SAFE PLACE.

A spotter views the area and chooses a safe place for the jumpers to land. The best place is a clearing a short hike from the fire, but not in front of it.

2. CHECK THE WIND.

The spotter also checks the direction and speed of the wind. The pilot then flies the plane to a place where the jumpers can use the wind to help them hit their landing zone.

3. JUMP.

The smoke jumpers exit the plane two at a time. This gets them out quickly but also in an orderly fashion so there are no collisions or tangling of parachutes.

Training / Montana

THE UNITED STATES HAS ABOUT 400 SMOKE JUMPERS. RUSSIA HAS 4,000.

Why such a difference? The greatest expanse of evergreen forest in the world stretches across northern Europe and Asia. This forest makes up half of Russia's territory—nearly two billion acres (809,371,285 ha). Smoke jumpers are the only defense against wildfires in this immense wilderness. During summer, the smoke jumpers scramble from fire to fire. They put them out quickly and in a surprisingly low-tech but effective way.

From the moment Russian smoke jumpers hit the ground, they become almost completely self-sufficient. They may even make some of their own equipment. One of the first things these jumpers might do is cut tree branches or saplings to construct handles for their shovels and axe heads. Backfires can be lit with matches and flaming strips of birch bark. If flames are low and creeping, firefighters simply shovel dirt on them or stamp them out with ever-green boughs. It's simple but effective.

Putting out the fire is only half the adventure. Because it's difficult to transport supplies over such a vast area, Russian smoke jumpers sometimes have to find their own food. My group of jumpers carried hunting and fishing gear. And when the fishing pole got lost? No problem. They just cut a sapling, attached some string, and tied on a piece of sharp metal for a fishhook.

Wilderness skills like these are essential for these smoke jumpers, because they may be camping in the woods long after the fire is out. Aircraft fuel can be scarce, so a helicopter pickup may be a week or more away. Although Russian smoke jumpers don't always have the latest high-tech resources, they successfully battle fire with skill and determination.

Smoke jumpers in the United States board a Short C-23 Sherpa.

Notes From the Field

FROM 1993 TO 2000, the United States and Russia took part in a firefighting exchange program in which the two countries exchanged several smoke jumpers for a fire season. It was a chance to share techniques and experiences. I've met Russian smoke jumpers who are impressed with some modern American equipment. I've met American smoke jumpers that admire Russian resourcefulness. All of the firefighters share a strong sense of pride and satisfaction in their work, no matter where it takes them.

**Russian firefighters
at rest and at work**

THE WINDS WERE CALM.

Flames only a foot high crept gently through dry grass beneath gnarled oak trees. I listened to the crackling of the fire and the scraping of shovels and Pulaskis against the ground. It was as quiet and peaceful as a fire could be. "There's not much to photograph here," I said to myself. "This fire is done."

That was late in the afternoon. I had been shooting photos of a small crew of firefighters tackling the last bit of fire on a hillside in California's Napa Valley. Strong winds the night before had pushed the fire toward homes. Unfortunately, a couple of them had burned. A crew had worked tirelessly during the night to widen a fire line. These efforts had limited the damage and kept the fire in check.

Suddenly, without warning, the roar of airplane engines boomed directly overhead. Out of the corner of my eye, I saw a huge plane barely skimming the treetops. We all looked up. The sky was reddish pink ... and it was falling!

We knew what it was. The plane had just dropped its entire load of fire retardant on the flames—and on us. At first it felt like heavy rain. Then ... WHUMPH! The rest of the load slammed us. It was like being clobbered with 2,000 gallons (7,571 L) of cool, thick salad dressing. I was covered from head to toe with the stuff. Good thing my mouth had been closed.

Good thing, too, I had my camera ready. I photographed the entire gooey episode as it unfolded before me—or rather, all over me, and everyone else. The retardant did its job all right; it put the fire out. But we had never gotten word to clear the area before the drop. Sometimes communication glitches happen. Fortunately, this one wasn't serious, and a hot shower washed away the mess. My camera? It hasn't been the same since.

FIREfact

THE FIRE CREW that had worked through the night to widen the fire line in the Napa fire was made up of prison inmates. The California Department of Forestry has about 200 inmate fire crews. Some other states also use inmate crews to help fight wildfires.

HEADS UP

A plane douses flames with fire retardant in California.

RIGHT: Unlucky firefighters are caught in a retardant drop in California.

the AIRShow

DC-IO tankers can carry and deliver fire retardant or water.

DURING A FIRE, AIRCRAFT DO MORE THAN CARRY FIREFIGHTERS AND EQUIPMENT.

Planes called air tankers dump water and other liquids on a fire to help snuff it out. These planes sometimes work in pairs, with one flying a few minutes behind the other.

Imagine walking along a lake and seeing an air tanker suddenly appear over the horizon. The plane banks sharply, levels off, and swoops down over the water. The tanker gently touches down on the lake, but it doesn't land. Instead, it skims across the water's surface. As it does, a couple thousand gallons of water are forced into a tank in the belly of the aircraft. About 15 seconds later, the plane rises back into the sky and heads toward the wildfire. It's quite a show, and it's just beginning.

As the tanker flies off, another one circles around, descends toward the water, fills up, and lifts off. Both air tankers dump their water on the fire and then return for refills.

Air tankers can keep up these water drops for hours. The water usually doesn't put out the roaring flames, but it does cool them enough to make them smaller and slower. This buys precious time for hotshots and other ground crews to dig line and gain control of the fire.

Besides water, some planes are equipped with tanks of fire retardant, like the chemical mix that splattered the fire crew and me in Napa Valley. Firefighters call it red mud or sky Jell-O. It's a thick liquid gel that can be dropped directly onto the fire to cool it or in front of the fire to form a barrier against it. As a barrier, the gel coats the vegetation so that it doesn't ignite quickly when the flames reach the treated area. The gel is dyed red so that pilots can see where it's already been dropped. After the fire, some chemicals in the retardant act as fertilizer to help new plants grow.

WILDFIRE AIR FLEET

FROM SINGLE ENGINE PLANES to jumbo jets, many kinds of aircraft are used around the world to fight wildfires. Here's a small sampling.

TWIN COMMANDER 600

This plane carries the Air Tactical Group Supervisor (ATGS). Called Air Tactical or Air Attack, the plane flies above other aircraft so that the ATGS can coordinate their movements in fighting the fire.

SHORT C-23 SHERPA

This plane from Northern Ireland is one of several kinds of aircraft that deliver smoke jumpers and cargo to remote wildfires.

ERICKSON S-64 AIR CRANE

This helicopter becomes a helitanker when fitted with a tank for carrying water. A snorkel hangs down so the copter can fill with water while hovering above a lake, river, or other source.

BOMBARDIER CL-415 SUPERSCOOPER

This large Canadian air tanker scoops up to 1,621 gallons (6,140 L) of water as it skims the surface of a lake, ocean, or other water body.

AIR TRACTOR AT-802

This Single Engine Air Tanker (SEAT) is a crop duster that has been adapted for fighting fires. This highly maneuverable aircraft delivers 800 gallons (3,028 L) of water or retardant with pinpoint accuracy.

ANTONOV AN-2

This Russian biplane can fly slower than other single engine planes, which increases the accuracy of its drops.

BEECHCRAFT KING AIR 90

A twin engine lead plane like this one guides an air tanker to its drop zone. The lead plane releases white smoke to show the tanker where to drop the fire retardant.

MCDONNELL DOUGLAS DC-10

This aircraft used to be one of the largest airliners in the sky. Now it's the largest air tanker in the world currently in use. It can deliver up to 12,000 gallons (45,000 L) of fire retardant in a path one mile (1.6 km) long and 300 feet (91 m) wide.

FIREfact

YOU MIGHT THINK that attacking fire from the air is free of risk. But there's no such thing when it comes to firefighting. In fact, from 1990 through 2006, nearly a fourth of the 310 deaths of wildland firefighters in the United States came from aircraft accidents.

HIGH-TECH EYES
IN THE SKY

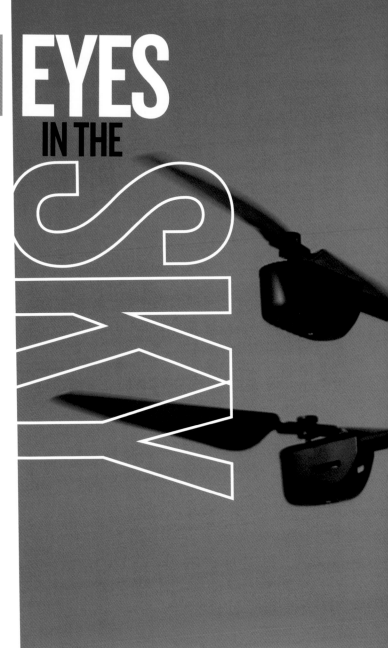

PLANES AND HELICOPTERS PROVIDE A BIRD'S-EYE VIEW

of a wildfire's movements, the lay of the land, and power lines that might be in the way. This information is critical for firefighters on the ground. But as you know, wildfire conditions change constantly. Piloted aircraft can't be in the air every minute to monitor the fire. It's too expensive and too risky. That's where drones come in.

Drones are small, remotely controlled aircraft that can stay in the air for many hours at a time. Video cameras on the drones can be the firefighters' eyes in the sky. Drones also can provide Internet service by hovering over wireless "dead zones" in rugged terrain. This is a big help when firefighters need to communicate by phone and gather up-to-date weather information. Drones have been used successfully in battling some fires. They may become increasingly important for firefighting as people learn how best to apply this new technology.

In addition to eyes in the sky, firefighters use eyes in space—satellites. Some satellites have sensors that show sources of heat on Earth's surface. The satellites can view large areas of the globe at once. They have detected fires in places not covered by lookouts or planes, such as remote areas of Alaska, U.S.A.

In Canada, a system called REMSAT (Real Time Emergency Management via Satellite) tracks every aircraft, engine, and fire crew in real time on a computer screen. Ground crews use handheld devices to send and receive text messages about their progress. They also can message for help if problems arise.

Satellites and drones can be important technologies for fighting fires. But no matter how high-tech the tools get, the main weapon against a blazing wildfire is still the firefighter on the ground with a simple, low-tech hand tool.

A drone gives firefighters a bird's-eye view of a wild-fire in Sierra de Bahoruco, Dominican Republic.

FIREsmarts

WITH ALL THE PEOPLE AND VEHICLES in the air and on the ground, communication is key to fighting a fire safely. In fact, communication is key in any situation that could become dangerous; this applies to anyone, not just firefighters. If you are going somewhere to play, explore, or even run an errand, be sure to tell a parent or guardian where you'll be and for how long. Get permission. Avoid going places alone. Carry a phone, and make sure it's charged and that it works in the area where you will be. Keep in contact while you are away, even if there's nothing wrong. This is one way you can be just like a wildland firefighter.

NATURE'S SIGNAL

AFTER AIR AND GROUND CREWS have worked together to put out a wildfire, the question may remain: How did the fire start? The answer usually is not obvious. Unless people witnessed the moment the fire started and reported it, fire investigators need to do some first-class sleuthing.

But before they figure out *how* the fire started, they have to determine *where* it started. It may seem like an impossible task. Yet experienced investigators can observe thousands of acres of charred wilderness and trace the fire back to a spot the size of a dinner plate. How do they do it? One method is to follow natural clues and look for patterns. For example, wildfire usually spreads outward in a V pattern from the point of origin. Aerial photos can show this pattern. The fire's origin may be near the base of the V.

See the How-To feature at the end of this chapter for other ways that investigators figure out where and how wildfires start.

63

MANN GULCH

THE FIRE WAS SPOTTED AROUND NOON ON AUGUST 5, 1949.

It was burning on the forested ridge of the south slope of Mann Gulch. This small, steep valley, or gulch, leads down a mountainside to the Missouri River in Montana's Helena National Forest. Around 4 p.m., 15 smoke jumpers parachuted into the gulch, landing about a half mile from the fire. They met up with the forest ranger who had reported the fire and who had been fighting it alone the past four hours.

The fire was too intense to attack from the front. So the crew leader ordered the firefighters to move to the north slope and head down the gulch toward the river. From there, they intended to fight the fire more safely along its flank.

As the crew hiked down the gulch, they were unaware that gusty winds had blown embers off the flaming forest onto the lower reaches of the north slope. Several spot fires had sprung up in the trees, brush, and grass between the crew and the river. The spots quickly grew and joined forces. Strong winds pushed this swelling wall of flame up the gulch toward the firefighters coming down. But because of the rugged terrain, they couldn't see it. They didn't know that they were walking right into the teeth of the fiery beast. It was 5:40.

At 5:45 they saw it. Wagner Dodge, the crew leader, ordered the men to drop their tools and run back up the gulch as fast as they could.

The fire was the length of a football field behind them and closing fast. Dodge knew they couldn't outrun it. So he did something that no professional firefighter had ever done before. He made an escape fire. He took out a match and lit the grass in front of him. The flames quickly burned out a large patch up the side of the slope. Dodge stepped into the black. He directed others to join him but they couldn't hear him, and they didn't understand what he was doing. They continued to run up the gulch with 50-foot (15-m) flames rolling toward them like a tidal wave.

Two of the smoke jumpers managed to make it to the top of the rocky ridge and take refuge amid the rocks on the other side. They survived. So did Dodge, who laid face down in the charred grass as the larger fire barreled around his safety zone. The passing flames were so hot that the rising air actually lifted him off the ground several times.

Investigators survey the site of Dodge's escape fire in 1949.

Within two minutes of passing Dodge, the flames caught up with the other 13 firefighters. Their deaths were tragic. Yet out of this tragedy came new hope.

The Mann Gulch Fire led to further research, safety guidelines, and training techniques that have benefited firefighters ever since. Fire shelters were invented, and safety guidelines urged firefighters to stay aware of changing conditions, identify escape routes and safety zones, and maintain communication. (The Mann Gulch smoke jumpers didn't have a radio because it had broken during the cargo drop.) Partly as a result of this tragic fire, today's firefighters know much more about how to recognize dangerous situations and how to avoid them.

Smoke jumpers / 1941

HELENA

MANN GULCH

NATIONAL

Helena ★

FOREST

Missouri

Smith

Clark Fork

Canyon Ferry Lake

0   25 miles

0   25 kilometers

British Columbia / Canada

HOW TO DETERMINE ORIGIN & CAUSE

A WILDFIRE TYPICALLY SPREADS outward in a V pattern. The point, or base, of the charred V-shaped landscape is a good place to search for the fire's origin and cause. But no single clue is foolproof.

Fire investigators look for different clues, like those described below, as they walk through the charred remains of a wildfire. They also talk to people who may have seen the fire in its early stages. Then they put all this information together to form a scenario of how the fire started and spread.

When investigators have narrowed the search for the fire's origin to a small area, maybe the size of a backyard, they can start looking for the cause. A ring of rocks might point to an unattended campfire as the culprit. A downed power line or damaged transformer might mean electrical sparks were the cause. Was lightning reported in the area? A gash in a tree trunk could show where a bolt started the blaze.

Little escapes the fire investigator's keen observations. After a fire burned 137,000 acres (55,442 ha) near Denver, Colorado, U.S.A., an inspector discovered three matches at the point of origin. Later, an arsonist admitted to setting the fire. The evidence was there. The evidence is almost always there. Fire investigators use incredible patience, perseverance, skill, and knowledge to find it.

TREE DAMAGE	GRASS DAMAGE	FIRE SHADOWS	NONCOMBUSTIBLE OBJECTS	LIMITED DAMAGE
Tree damage usually is greater on the side that faced the approaching flames. So the more heavily charred sides of the tree trunks point toward the area of origin.	As fire burns through tall grass, the bases of the stems burn first. Without the support, the upper stems fall over. Stems that fall forward get burned as the fire passes over them. But stems that fall backward often escape the flames, which have already passed. Therefore, unburned grass stems on the ground may point toward the fire's origin.	A fire shadow is a small area of unburned or lightly burned grass that was protected from burning because it's next to a rock or other object. If a fire shadow is on one side of a rock, the fire came from the opposite direction. Fire shadows are more common where the fire started because that's where and when the fire was coolest and less likely to burn all the way around rocks.	Rocks won't burn up in a wildfire, but they may have burn stains or soot on the side that faced the approaching fire.	When a fire begins, it hasn't yet generated a lot of heat. So the middle and upper reaches of trees may show less damage near the origin even though trees farther away are completely burned.

YOUR TURN TO INVESTIGATE

A WILDFIRE has just been extinguished, and you are called in to investigate how it started. See how well you can interpret the clues.

Firefighters mop up.

1. Look at this drawing of a burned forest. Where do you think the fire started?

2. From which direction did the fire come?

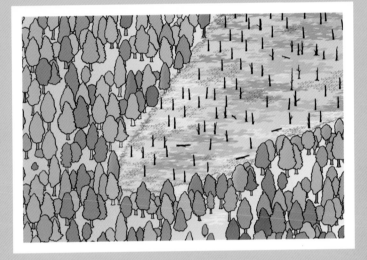

3. You see a lot of these in one area. What are they? What do they mean?

4. Can you find evidence of how the fire started? Look closely.

Crown fire in Yoho National
Park, British Columbia

CHAPTER 4

>>> # Ecology
of a
Wildfire

[Ecology—The study of how living things interact with one another and their environment; Ecosystem—All the living and non-living things that interact in an environment, such as a forest or prairie]

KILLER BEETLES

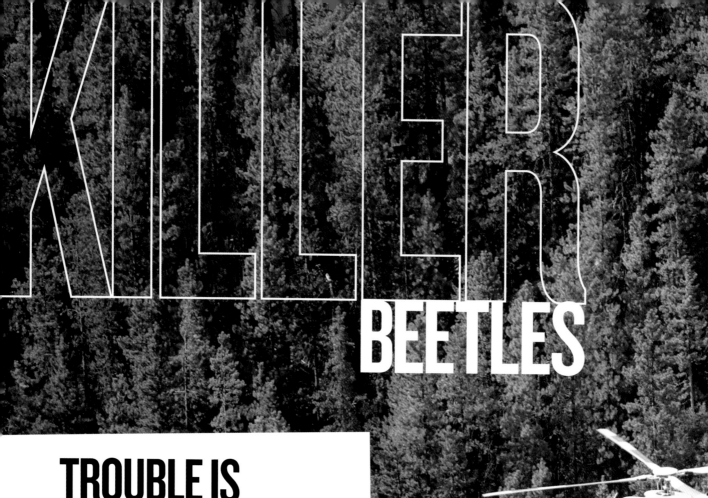

TROUBLE IS BREWING IN THE FORESTS, AND IT'S NOT FROM FIRE. IN FACT, IT'S PARTLY FROM A LACK OF FIRE.

The problem became clear to me in the spring of 2007 as I traveled into the Black Hills National Forest in South Dakota with a ranger from the U.S. Forest Service. On either side of the road, thousands of ponderosa pines stood dead or dying. Their once healthy green needles were now reddish brown, and some trees were almost bare. Soon their bark would fall away, leaving behind stands of dead, ghostly gray trees. The killer? An insect no bigger than a grain of rice—the mountain pine beetle.

To get a closer look, we walked over to a tree that to me seemed perfectly healthy. But the ranger pointed out the symptom of a sick tree. Little structures that looked like white, partly melted birthday candles were sticking out of the bark. These are called pitch tubes. When the beetles bore through the bark, the tree tries to defend itself by pushing a thick liquid called pitch out through the holes. The idea is to kick the beetles out along with the pitch.

But it's a losing battle. By the time you see pitch tubes, it's too late. The tree is doomed.

The forest ranger showed me why. He took out a knife, cut into a section of bark, and peeled it back. Beneath it were numerous tunnels running up and down the wood. During the summer and fall, adult beetles dig the tunnels by eating the wood. Then they lay their eggs in the tunnels. When the eggs hatch, the young beetles—called grubs—further excavate tunnels. All of these tunnels cut off the flow of food within the tree, from the needles to the roots. In addition, the adult beetles spread a fungus that blocks the flow of water from the roots to the needles. The tree dies within a year.

By the next summer, the grubs will have become adult beetles. They will emerge from the dead tree and fly off to find another host. When they find a suitable tree, the beetles will give off a chemical that attracts other beetles. It's like yelling, "Hey, everyone, come over here! I found a tree we can live in!" Hundreds of thousands of beetles will attack the tree, and the cycle will start again.

It's quite a buggy problem, and a lack of fire has helped cause it. Fires used to burn through these pine forests every few years. The flames were low, and most of the trees survived. But the frequent fires provided enough heat to keep the pesky beetle population from getting too big. There was a balance of nature.

But throughout most of the 20th century, fire policy in the United States and elsewhere helped throw this balance out of whack. The policy was to put out every fire as soon as possible. That may seem like a good idea at first, but it has actually taken away one of the beetles' enemies. Without fire, bark beetles like these flourish. Fortunately, people now realize that wildfire plays a major role in keeping forests and other ecosystems healthy.

Pine beetle channels

Pine beetles

Firefighters prevent the spread of mountain pine beetles through a controlled burn in Yoho National Park, British Columbia.

Notes From the Field

YOU KNOW THAT PRESCRIBED BURNS are used to fight fire with fire. Sometimes prescribed burns are also used to fight beetles. In Alberta, Canada, I watched as firefighters set 5,000 acres (2,023 ha) of lodgepole pines ablaze in Yoho National Park. The purpose was to stop the spread of bark beetles. It worked! The burn created a buffer zone that stopped the beetles from spreading into other areas of the forest. But the bark beetle problem will continue in northern forests, not only because of lack of fire but also because of climate change. In the past, bitter cold winters killed off much of the beetle population. Now, more of the beetles survive through the warmer winters.

LIFE RETURNS TO THE FOREST

FIRE CHANGES AN ECOSYSTEM. HOWEVER, NOT ALL OF THE CHANGES MAY BE WHAT YOU'D EXPECT.

Imagine a burned-out forest. A year ago, this ecosystem was lush and green, rich with life. Then a fire roared through. Afterward, charred trees stood like black pipes. The branches that remained stretched out like crooked fingers. Ash blanketed the forest floor. In this landscape of black and gray, it looked like nothing would ever grow here again. But looks can be deceiving.

Seeds and roots buried in the soil were unharmed by the fire. More seeds blew in on the wind and settled to the ground. Within two weeks, light green blades of grass poked through the ash. Tiny stems popped up and uncurled the first delicate leaves of new pine trees. Birch stems shot up from the bases of burned trunks. Shrubs and wildflowers sprouted next to scorched fallen timber.

Every day brought growth and the sight of something new. Fireweed and geraniums opened their pinkish purple flowers. Other flowers followed. Soon the forest floor burst into a carpet of color.

Plants attracted animals. Insects crawled out of the ground to feed on fresh leaves and the pollen of flowers. Mice left their underground burrows to nibble on sprouts and seeds. But they had to watch out for the hungry hawks perched on the burned branches. Other birds returned to feed on the insects. Large animals like deer and elk came back to graze on fresh grass, shoots, and leaves.

A forest shows new growth after a fire.

1-2-3 HABITAT!

FIRE DOESN'T SWEEP through an entire ecosystem at once. A few small sections may burn one year, and a few others the next, and still other sections several years later. Some parts will remain unburned for decades. The result is a healthy patchwork of many different habitats, or places where organisms live, within an ecosystem. Here are three of those patches. Each one represents a major stage of growth after a fire in a forest ecosystem.

1. NEW GROWTH
In the weeks and months after a fire, a lush mixture of plants grows in areas that are now more open to sunshine. These plants include grasses, wildflowers, shrubs, and saplings.

2. YOUNG FOREST
Several years after a fire, trees have grown taller than other plants. The trees form a dense young forest that shades the forest floor and prevents many other plants from growing.

3. OLD-GROWTH FOREST
Many small fires may have burned along the floor of an old forest, but the trees have survived for decades or even centuries. Some of the trees die with age and fall. Or storms blow them down, creating clearings and meadows.

FIREfact

WHEN YOU HEAR about wildfires, do you ever wonder what happens to the animals? Most birds fly away to safety. Squirrels, deer, coyotes, and most other mammals flee in time to escape the flames. Groundhogs and mice stay safe in underground burrows. So do most reptiles, like snakes and lizards. Insects seek safety underground, too. Frogs and other amphibians seek water or dig into mud on the side of a river. Sadly, some animals do die in the fire, but most escape unharmed. And sometimes, in the midst of battling the raging flames, firefighters are able to lend a hand to a furry friend. Such was the case in 2015 when firefighters found an injured koala at the base of a tree during an Australian bushfire. The koala—named Jeremy after his rescuer—was treated for burns on his paws and released back into the wild a few weeks later.

By next year, the forest will have changed even more. Saplings of aspen, birch, and pine will be chest-high. Huckleberry and other berry bushes will have grown in the sun-drenched clearings created by the fire, and these will have brought the bears. Bears love berries, and they know that the best places to find these sweet treats are in areas that recently burned.

Over the next few years, dozens more plants and animals will return to the forest. Again it will be lush and green, full of life. The fire won't have destroyed it at all. In fact, fire is a helpful and necessary part of this forest ecosystem.

WHAT'S GOOD ABOUT WILDFIRE?

DO YOU RECYCLE?

Maybe you have bins at home or school for aluminum cans, glass, and paper. These items are broken down and processed so that the materials they are made of can be used again. It's a great idea, but people can't take all the credit. We're only following nature's lead.

Nature constantly recycles. Just dig up a handful of soil and take a good look. You might notice bits of plants, like a mushy piece of twig or a section of leaf so thin you can see through it. These plant parts are in the process of decomposing, or rotting. This means they are breaking down and returning to the soil. It's nature's way of recycling the nutrients and other materials that make up the plants so they can be used again.

Decomposition is part of a healthy ecosystem. So is fire. In fact, fire helps things decompose. In wet climates, a log decomposes fairly quickly. Thirty years after a tree falls, you might not even recognize the crumbly mass that used to be a log. Moss, worms, insects, mushrooms, and bacteria are

The aftermath of a fire near Hayfork, California

BENEFITS OF WILDFIRE

ARE YOU SURPRISED that fire is one of nature's best recyclers? Here are some more answers to the question: What's good about wildfire?

> Frequent fires that burn close to the ground reduce the amount of brush, logs, and fallen branches and leaves on the forest floor without harming larger, healthy trees. This keeps fuel from building up, which helps prevent larger, more destructive fires.

> Fire opens a dense forest so that more sunlight reaches the forest floor. This allows the growth of a variety of plants that provide food and shelter for many kinds of animals.

> Small fires create "edges" in an ecosystem. An edge is a border between two areas that have different kinds of plant life, such as a meadow and a forest, or different ages of plants, such as a young forest and an old-growth forest. Edges provide a lot of different resources and habitats for wildlife.

> Ashes from a fire act as fertilizer, which nourishes the soil and helps plants grow.

> Fire removes pests and diseased plants from an ecosystem.

> Fire removes invasive plants. These are plants that do not usually grow in an area and that compete with native plants for nutrients and space.

> In grasslands, fire removes woody plants, such as shrubs and trees, that compete with the native grasses and wildflowers. The grasses and wildflowers burn, too, but they quickly grow back, healthier than ever.

among the decomposers that break down the log and release the nutrients into the soil. The enriched soil helps new plants grow.

In dry climates, however, a log might take a couple hundred years to decompose. Fire speeds up the process. Burning breaks down plants quickly and releases nitrogen and other nutrients into the soil.

Fire is important to the health of many ecosystems. That makes sense. After all, fire is a natural part of many ecosystems, just like water, sunshine, soil, and living things. And every part plays a role in keeping an ecosystem healthy.

Cascades / Washington, U.S.A.

BUILT FOR FIRE

Bicknell's geranium

Chamerion angustifolium, also known as fireweed, is one of the first plants to colonize an area after a fire.

A CERTAIN PURPLE FLOWER BLOOMS IN NORTHERN FORESTS, GROWING ON LONG, HAIRY STEMS. It's called Bicknell's geranium, or Bicknell's cranesbill. If you happen to see this flower among the aspen, spruce, or fir trees, you know two things. One, a fire swept through the area within the past few years. Two, the seeds from which these flowering plants grew were likely in the soil for decades, and maybe for more than 100 years.

Bicknell's geranium has a very special quality. Its seeds germinate, or begin to grow, only after a fire. Heat triggers the growth. This heat comes from the fire passing over the soil and from the sun warming the soil after fire has removed overlying twigs, leaves, and shrubs. The plants grow, bloom, and then release seeds.

After several years, other plants grow large enough to block the geraniums' sunlight. The geraniums die in the constant shade, but their seeds are still in the soil. There they lie dormant, not growing but still alive. Then one day—maybe 50, 100, or 150 years in the future—another fire passes through. Guess what? The seeds germinate, and the geraniums once again show their flowery faces to the sun.

Living things are adapted to their ecosystem. This means they have traits, or qualities, that allow them to survive the conditions in that ecosystem, including fire. Seeds of fireweed, for example, just like Bicknell's geranium, can lie dormant for years until fire clears away competing plants and triggers growth.

NATURE'S SIGNAL

WHEN A TREE IS CUT DOWN, a careful observer can tell how many times the tree survived a fire. Look closely at the rings. Each ring shows a year of growth as the tree added another layer of cells to its width. Among the tree rings are dark notches called fire scars. These are layers of charcoal that formed as fire penetrated the bark and burned part of the living tissue beneath. The tree continued to grow around the charcoal, leaving the scar as a record of the fire. Some 1,000-year-old ponderosa pines have 100 fire scars. The scars provide a history of fire in that area, showing when fires burned through and how intense they were.

Fynbos regrowth
after a fire in
South Africa

PLANT ADAPTATIONS TO FIRE

BICKNELL'S GERANIUM has adapted to fire by using its heat to trigger growth. Here are some other amazing ways plants are adapted to fire. Some of these plants depend on fire to even exist.

GIANT SEQUOIA

Giant sequoias can reach more than 300 feet (91 m) in height, but they need fire to get a good start in life. Fire clears the forest floor so that sequoia seedlings can grow in the full sunlight they need. The flames don't harm the adult trees—not with a tough protective bark that is up to 2 feet (0.6 m) thick!

PONDEROSA PINE

Ponderosa pines have thick bark to protect the living wood beneath the bark from fire. These trees also shed their lower limbs as they grow. This prevents fire from climbing the tree and reaching the needles.

LODGEPOLE PINE CONE

The cones of some trees—like jack pines, lodgepole pines, and black spruce—are coated and sealed with a tough, waxy resin. It takes the heat of a fire to melt this resin. Then the cones open and the seeds fall onto the ash, where they grow without competition from grasses and other plants.

CEANOTHUS CHAPARRAL

Some kinds of plants found in the chaparral, like ceanothus, have leaves coated with a flammable resin. The resin helps fuel fire. This is good for the plant because, like Bicknell's geranium, the ceanothus's seeds need intense heat to germinate. The adult plants above ground burn up in seconds, but the roots resprout quickly after the fire.

PRAIRIE GRASS

Prairie grasses grow back from underground roots, which remain alive after a fire passes.

FIRE LILY

Like Bicknell's geranium, fire lily seeds lie dormant in the soil until fire clears out the vegetation above. Then the lilies bloom within a couple weeks. The quick flowering time lets the lilies be among the first plants to sprout and make seeds before most other plants start growing and competing for resources.

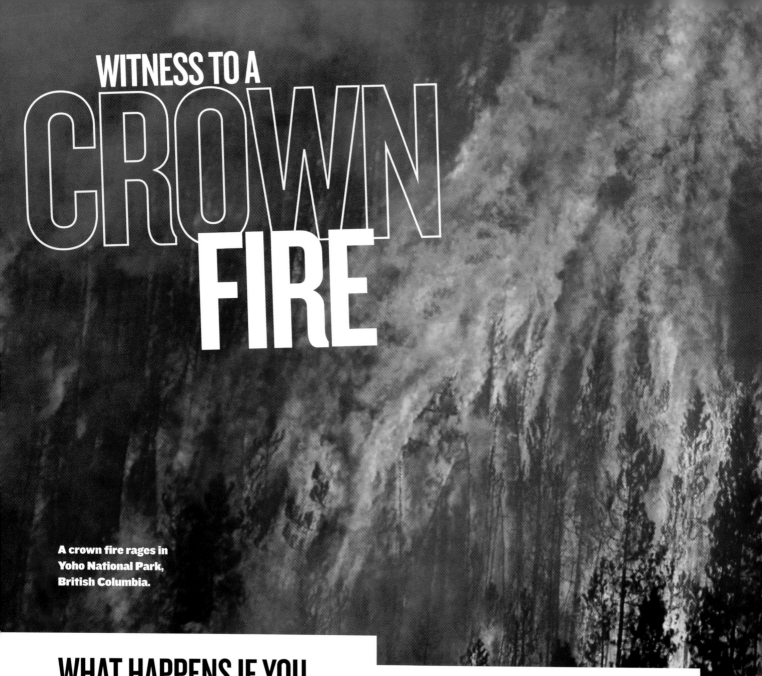

WITNESS TO A CROWN FIRE

A crown fire rages in Yoho National Park, British Columbia.

WHAT HAPPENS IF YOU PLANT A VEGETABLE GARDEN BUT DON'T TAKE CARE OF IT?

In a couple of weeks, dandelions, grass, and other unwanted plants sprout among the young tomato and pepper plants. The roots of the weeds draw water and nutrients away from the vegetables, making the weeds grow tall and crowding out the veggies. Soon your garden is nothing more than a patch of weeds, and the only way to grow vegetables is to dig everything up and start over.

But if you weed the garden regularly, the vegetable plants grow strong and the garden stays healthy. In a sense, fire is nature's way of weeding many of Earth's natural gardens—that is, many of its ecosystems. You already know that low-intensity ground fire cleans up a forest floor by removing bushes, small trees, and dead vegetation. The mature trees survive and grow healthier in the nourishing ash.

But if a forest hasn't burned regularly, then bushes and saplings grow tall and dense between the existing mature trees. Over time, this new growth, as well as any dead vegetation that piles up, fills the empty spaces in the forest. When a fire occurs, the flames use this vegetation as bridges, or ladders, to climb up into the canopy of the forest. The result is a crown fire—a devastating fire that jumps from treetop to treetop.

Notes From the Field

THE AFTEREFFECTS OF A CROWN FIRE CAN BE DEVASTATING. Few, if any, trees survive. Organic matter in the soil may burn to a depth of several inches. The soil becomes like moon dust—fine, gray ash that rises and hangs in the air with each footstep. Eventually, rain washes this fine ash into streams, which damages the habitat for fish and other freshwater life. The forest ecosystem will recover, even from a crown fire, but it will take a while. It's like digging up your garden and starting over.

A crown fire can destroy everything in its path. I know from firsthand experience.

I was photographing fires from a helicopter as we flew across the mountains of central Idaho one day during a fire season some years back. The weather favored wildfire—hot, dry, and windy. Smoke rose from several fires all across the landscape. In some places, the smoke took the shape of billowing mushroom clouds, signaling especially intense fires.

We flew near one of these clouds. Beneath the smoke was a raging crown fire a half mile wide. It was unlike any other kind of wildfire I had experienced.

The flames took giant leaps from crown to crown, as if the fire were running across the tops of the trees. Sounds were muffled because I was wearing earphones, but a crown fire roars like a freight train.

The size of the flames was incredible. I had to remind myself that I was looking down on trees that were 150 feet (46 m) tall. Yet, they were dwarfed by flames that reached 200 feet (61 m) into the air.

Crown fires this fierce are impossible to stop. Once the fire is in the crown, or leafy treetop, and the wind is pushing it, the flames easily reach over any fire line into the next stand of trees. All firefighters can do is wait for the weather to change and the flames to run out of fuel.

RETHINKING THE WAR ON FIRE

LOOK BACK THROUGH THIS BOOK FOR DESCRIPTIONS OF WILDFIRE AND HOW PEOPLE RESPOND TO IT.

You'll see words like *raging*, *front*, *battle*, *fight*, and *attack*. Sounds like a war, doesn't it? In a way, it is a war—a war on fire.

The war on fire started after the deadly 1910 Big Blowup. The U.S. Forest Service decided that the best way to prevent large, devastating fires was to put out every fire, big or small, as quickly as possible. In fact, in 1935 the Forest Service started a "10 a.m. policy," which set a goal of containing and controlling a fire by 10:00 the morning after it was reported. That goal wasn't always met, but it shows that the war against fire was on in a big way.

Fighting wildfire became the Forest Service's main mission for much of the 20th century. Forest agencies in some other countries also followed the policy of putting out all fires. In addition, most of the public thought all wildfires should be extinguished as quickly as possible.

Not everyone agreed. Some people understood the ecological importance of wildfire. For example, for

centuries Native Americans on the plains had burned sections of prairie every year or so to keep the ecosystem free of invasive brush and trees. The grasses grew back the next year and attracted ducks, buffalo, and other animals that these Native Americans hunted.

Over the decades, firefighters bravely faced flames, skillfully extinguishing most fires before they could burn through the forests. In the meantime, the forests filled in. Brush and small trees grew in the open spaces among the large trees. Leaves, logs, and branches cluttered the forest floor. This vegetation became ladder fuels that allowed flames to climb trees and produce larger blazes. In many cases, what would have been healthy ground fires became explosive crown fires.

Today, managers of wildlands recognize the benefits of wildfire: that fire destroys but also restores. Now managers are using prescribed fires (small, controlled burns) to clear out the buildup of fuels.

A quick evacuation is necessary after fire jumps the road in **Seeley Lake, Montana.**

NATURE'S SIGNAL

WHAT HAPPENS WHEN FIRE IS REMOVED FROM AN ECOSYSTEM THAT DEPENDS ON IT? COMPARE THESE PHOTOS OF THE SAME PLACE OVER THE YEARS.

1890
When low-intensity ground fires burned freely through the forest, this area of ponderosa pines contained 30 trees per acre.

1994
After about a hundred years of extinguishing fires as much as possible, the same area contained 1,800 trees per acre. This was nature's signal of an imbalance in the ecosystem.

1995
A year later, the same area contained no live trees per acre. Can you guess why? A catastrophic fire wiped out everything.

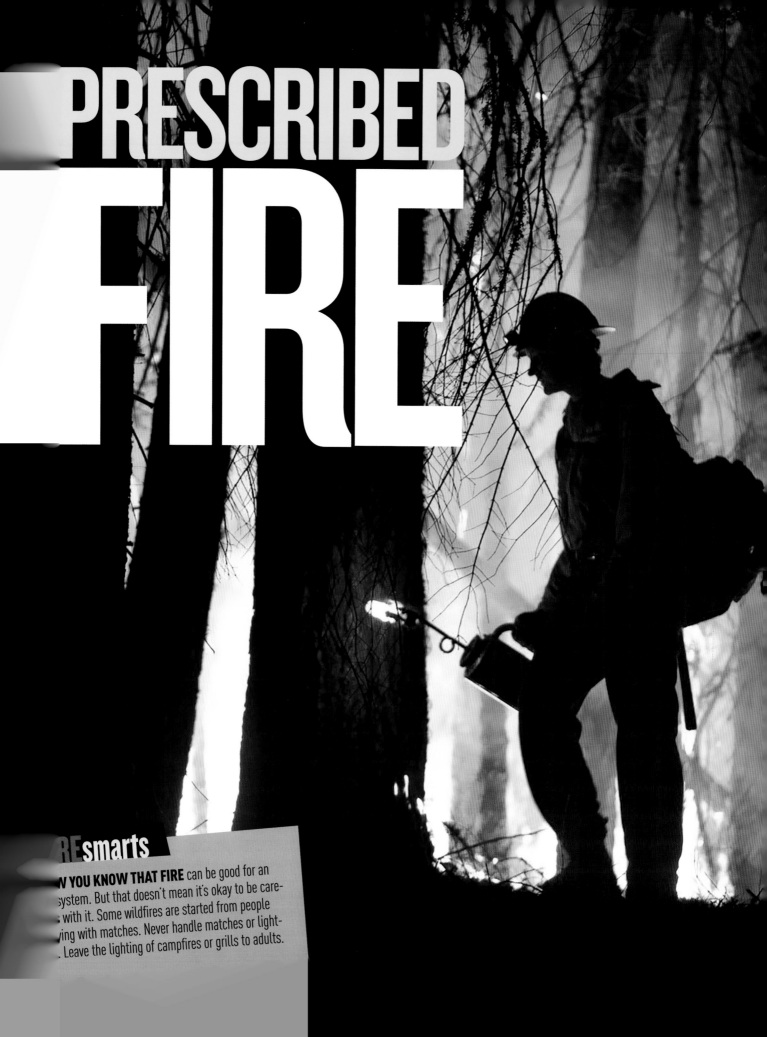

PRESCRIBED
FIRE

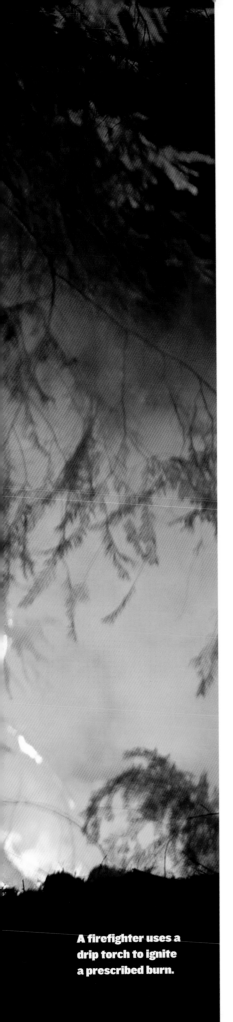

A firefighter uses a drip torch to ignite a prescribed burn.

A drip torch in use

PRESCRIBED FIRE IS AN
IMPORTANT TOOL

that can help restore a natural balance in ecosystems. But firefighters don't just light the grass and see what happens. A prescribed fire takes careful planning.

Everything has to be just right. Take the weather, for instance. If the weather is hot, dry, and windy, the fire manager, or person in charge, will call off the burn. If the fuels are too dry, a prescribed burn can spread too quickly and get out of control. So the manager might wait for rainy weather and do the burn a day or two later.

Laws about air quality may prevent a prescribed burn as well. Air pollution affects visibility and can make breathing difficult, especially for people who have breathing problems. Of course, fire smoke adds lots of pollution to the air. So if the air quality is already low, a prescribed burn will be delayed until air quality improves.

Fire managers also have to consider the shape of the land. Will the flames be moving uphill, downhill, over flat land, or over a combination of terrains? How will the wind direction affect the flames' movement over the terrain? The planning can get tricky. But a fire manager can analyze these and other factors and predict how long the fire will burn and even how high the flames will be.

Finally, when the many factors of weather, fuel, and air quality come together favorably, crews prepare for the prescribed burn. They dig a fire line around the burn area. They lay out hoses in case they need water to keep the fire under control, and for mop-up.

Firefighters then use drip torches to lay down lines of fire and start the burn. The drip torches drop small globs of flaming fuel—a mixture of diesel and gasoline—onto the grass. The fire will creep along the forest floor, engulfing small trees, downed branches, and logs. A separate fire crew will guard against any embers that might jump the fire line. Winds should be light. Yet the fire manager knows the wind can change speed and direction suddenly and make the fire burn out of control.

But most prescribed fires go as planned. The burn clears out the understory, or low-growing vegetation, in a specific part of the forest, greatly reducing the chances for a major fire later on. The burn opens spaces for native plants and enriches the soil. It's a small but important step toward restoring the balance of nature in the ecosystem.

YELLOWSTONE

TUCKED IN THE NORTHWEST CORNER OF WYOMING, U.S.A., IS A WONDERLAND OF NATURAL BEAUTY.

It's Yellowstone National Park. Here, you'll find magnificent waterfalls, towering geysers, colorful hot springs, and a variety of wildlife. You'll also see—here and there, amid the green forests—stands of dead lodgepole pines. These gray, barren poles are reminders of fires that swept through much of the park throughout the summer of 1988.

The spring of that year had been wetter than usual in Yellowstone. But by June, the rains had stopped, and Yellowstone became gripped in the worst drought in the park's history. Conditions were ripe for a big blaze. The lodgepole forests were hundreds of years old. Timber littered the ground. Grass had grown tall during the wet spring. Now all of this fuel was becoming bone-dry.

In the early summer, several thunderstorms produced no rain but plenty of lightning. The giant bolts of electricity ignited several fires within and just outside the park boundaries. At first, park officials were not very concerned. Although lightning had sparked 20 fires, they had been small, and 11 went out by themselves. Since 1972, the park had had a policy of letting wildfires burn as long as they were started naturally and did not threaten human life or property. So officials kept a close eye on the remaining fires and let them burn ... until mid-July.

That's when the decision was made to suppress, or put out, the fires, not only because of the continued dry conditions, but also because of pressure from the public and national media who were questioning the let-it-burn policy. A week later, things got out of control.

High winds drove the fires several miles a day. Flames jumped roads and fire lines. Flying embers started spot fires a mile (1.6 km) away. Other fires were popping up, and not all of them were from lightning. One large fire started when a tree fell on a power line. Another began from an unattended campfire. The largest fire ignited from a discarded cigarette. Throughout the summer, 50 fires burned within Yellowstone, and nearly 200 more burned just outside the park boundaries.

Massive efforts went into fighting the blazes. More than 25,000 firefighters from across the country took part. Their heroic efforts protected lives and property. But in the end, what put out the fires was the weather. In early September, cold temperatures, rain, and a dusting of snow doused the flames. By mid-November, all smoldering embers had been snuffed out.

Nearly a third of Yellowstone had been touched by fire. But fire is part of this ecosystem, and nature started recovering immediately. Colorful fireweed—often one of the first plants to grow after a fire—bloomed in a matter of days. Grizzly bears fed on the new vegetation and on the ants that took up residence in the burned wood. Elk returned to graze on the young aspen trees that sprouted in the freshly fertilized soil.

And today, beneath the dead lodgepole pines, another forest is growing. Crown fires provided the intense heat needed to open the cones of the mature lodgepoles and release their seeds. If not for that heat, the trees would likely have died of old age or disease without ever giving rise to the next generation.

So, like the gray, barren poles, the new growth is also a reminder of the Yellowstone fires, and how fire not only destroys but renews.

SPREAD THE WORD ABOUT WILDFIRE ECOLOGY

NOT ALL WILDFIRE IS BAD. That's an important message. It's a message that many people don't know or accept. How can you help people understand that some wildfire is necessary to restore and maintain balance within many ecosystems? Here are some basic steps:

1. Decide how to spread the word. You might choose one of these methods:
   - Create posters, flyers, or pamphlets.
   - Write and perform a poem, rap, or song.
   - Write and perform a skit or play.
   - Start a blog under an adult's guidance.
   - Post photos and videos accompanied by captions and commentary.

2. Conduct more research. This book is a great start, but also check out the resources listed on page 108.

3. Refine the message you want to send. Keep it simple, but provide evidence that supports your message.

> Here are some other great ways to share the message of wildfire ecology:
   - Give a presentation to your class on wildfires. Have your class write thank-you notes to firefighters and deliver them to your local fire station.
   - Write a letter to your mayor or governor.
   - Hold a bake sale with facts about wildfires to accompany each treat. Give the profits to your local fire station or a wildfire relief nonprofit organization.
   - Write a letter to your local newspaper.

Who knows?
Soon the message could be spreading like ... wildfire!

On a hilltop in the San Bernadino Mountains of California, all that remain of these homes after a fire are the burning gas lines.

CHAPTER 5

>>> **Living**
With
Wildfire

[Evacuate—Leave an area in
an organized way for safety;
Adapt—Change so as to live
with new conditions]

THE EMBER THAT GOT AWAY

WITH WILDFIRES, YOU NEVER KNOW WHAT YOU'RE GOING TO GET.

Every fire packs a surprise or two. Sometimes the surprise is gargantuan, like a sudden crown fire. Sometimes it's small and right at your feet.

Do you remember reading about the Eighth Street Fire outside Boise, Idaho? In chapter 1, I described how a crew of firefighters and I raced across a field to safety after the wind suddenly shifted. Well, the excitement didn't end there. On that same fire, late at night, I was photographing engine crews stretched along a highway. They had just lit a backfire on the north side of the road to burn up the brush between the road and the main fire. The backfire would eat up the main fire's fuel and stop it in its tracks.

That is, unless embers from the backfire happened to blow across the road. Then people's lives and property could be in danger. The highway was the only firebreak between the flames and homes. So crews kept their eyes on any embers that drifted up from the flames into the black midnight air.

Suddenly, an ember darted out of the flames. It moved quickly along the ground and up onto the road. It bolted back and forth and ran in circles around the firefighters. It was like the ember had legs. Then I realized—it did have legs!

An ember had fallen on the back of a rabbit. The poor creature was scared out of its wits and trying to shake loose from the glowing piece of wood. Firefighters tried to catch the rabbit and keep it from crossing the road into the unburned brush. If the ember started a spot fire there, the flames could spread to the homes.

Try as they might, the lunging firefighters were no match for the quick zigzags of the scared rabbit. It ran off into the inky blackness of the unburned brush. Everyone groaned. Two firefighters went after it but there were no signs of the ember or the rabbit. Fortunately, there were no signs of spot fires either.

Notes From the Field

ARE YOU WONDERING what happened to the rabbit and the glowing ember? Although we never found either one, the ember most likely fell off and went out by itself. The rabbit probably was unharmed. Its fur would have been thick enough to protect against the heat of an ember, even one that went on an unexpected piggyback ride.

Firefighters used flares to light these backfires during the Eighth Street Fire in Boise, Idaho.

91

THE WILDLAND URBAN INTERFACE

WILDLANDS ARE BEAUTIFUL PLACES.

That's why more and more people are choosing to live near them. From tall, deep forests to wide open prairies, people enjoy the peacefulness, natural beauty, and fresh air of these places.

For these and other reasons, suburbs expand farther and farther into the countryside. Housing subdivisions pop up near forests, prairies, and shrublands. Along with the homes come roads, schools, stores, and office buildings. The area where this development meets the natural ecosystem is called the wildland urban interface.

Sometimes the interface is clear to see. For example, a housing development might be built right up against a forest. Other times the interface is less obvious, like when houses are built within a forest or homes are built along streets that wind their way up wooded hills and canyons. In these cases, development and wilderness intermingle, or mix.

No matter what the wildland urban interface looks like, it puts a big strain on firefighters. In most cases, the development is in an ecosystem that depends on fires and is likely to get them. But when these fires flare up, instead of renewing the ecosystem, they threaten people's lives and livelihoods. So firefighters must do all they can to put the flames out.

Communities like these have magnificent views but must guard against wildfire.

However, buildings complicate things. One of the best ways to fight a wildfire is to set a backfire. But if that backfire is going to burn through a neighborhood, it's not an option. Firefighters have to use other methods. They might have to go house to house, spraying the outside walls with water or retardant to give the structure a fighting chance. They might scatter wood stacked against a house so that it doesn't act as fuel. They might fell nearby trees, dig line, and do small burnouts to clear a safety zone around a house or group of houses. These methods take precious time and often put firefighters in great danger.

OUR TURN TO ADAPT

IMAGINE MOVING INTO A HOUSE RIGHT ON THE BEACH ON THE GULF OF MEXICO. You can

play in the surf almost every day. The sounds are soothing, and the views are fantastic. What a dream come true! Yet it's not all fun in the sun.

Storms, including the occasional hurricane, are part of this coastal ecosystem, so your house may be built on stilts. This keeps towering storm waves from crashing through your living room. If a hurricane is coming, you might help your family nail large sheets of plywood over the windows to protect them from the storm's ferocious winds. You probably also have a plan in place to evacuate, or leave the area, before the hurricane strikes the coast. These are some of the ways that you can adapt, or make some changes, so that you can live with the storms.

Now imagine moving into a house surrounded by woods. Again, the sights and sounds of this ecosystem make every day an adventure. But you know that fire is also part of this forest ecosystem. Plants and animals that live here have adapted to the changes that fire brings. People who choose to live in fire-prone places can adapt, too. The graphic on the opposite page shows you how.

REDUCING FIRE RISK

REDUCING FIRE RISK

One way to adapt to wildfire is to reduce the risk of fire damage. Here are some steps caregivers and builders can take—with your help—to make houses and other buildings less vulnerable to fire.

1. Use fire-resistant roofing materials, such as ceramic or slate tiles or metal sheeting.

2. Place metal screens over vents to block embers from entering.

3. Trim tree branches so they don't overhang the house.

4. Cut tree limbs within 15 feet (4.6 m) of the ground.

5. Keep grass short and watered so that it doesn't become a prime fuel.

6. Clean up debris such as leaves and broken twigs.

7. Keep gutters clean of debris.

8. Space out trees and shrubs so that flames don't travel easily between them.

9. Call the power company to clear branches from power lines.

10. Keep firewood away from the house.

FIRE-ADAPTED COMMUNITIES

WHENEVER DISASTER STRIKES, COMMUNITIES PULL TOGETHER.

Whether the event was a tornado, earthquake, hurricane, flood, or fire, people pitch in to help one another rebuild and recover. It's amazing to see.

It's also terrific to see how communities can pull together to protect against disasters before they strike. That's what is happening in wildland urban interfaces across the country and around the world. People are helping one another live with wildfire. They do not depend on firefighters as their only protection. Instead, they work together to prevent human-caused wildfires and to reduce the risk of damage when fires occur. These motivated people are members of a growing number of fire-adapted communities.

The success of these communities depends on the involvement of each person living within them. Residents (even the kids), government agencies, firefighters, land developers, and businesses work together to create an environment that is compatible with wildfire. How do they do it?

The first big step is education. Many people who live in the wildland urban interface aren't aware of the wildfire risks. They don't know what you know from reading this book. Once they do learn how their decisions can decrease the risks, they're usually willing to take action.

And lots of people are willing to help. Firefighters and fire and building inspectors share ways to make homes and property more resistant to fire. Forest agencies may provide free chipping services to get rid of downed branches and brush. Neighbors share tips and costs for home improvements. Controlled burns keep the surrounding landscape from becoming overgrown with fuel.

A resident in Santa Clarita, California, saves what he can.

Two neighbors in Rancho Bernardo, California, embrace upon returning home after their evacuation.

Kids can help in lots of ways. They can learn more about reducing fire risks and spread the word. They can help with some of the hard work like restacking firewood or clearing away brush. Kids, and everyone else, can also help by following safety rules about wildfire, like the Fire Smarts tips in this book.

These and other actions really work. Fire-adapted communities experience far fewer wildfires caused by people than other areas do. They also suffer far less damage from fires and spend less money on firefighting efforts. Fire-adapted communities show that development can be compatible with wildfire.

Gear & Gadgets

SUPPOSE EMBERS FROM A WILDFIRE blow onto the roof and under the eaves of a house. The attic and top floor catch fire. People quickly become trapped in a second-story bedroom. How do they escape? The safest way is to deploy an escape ladder. The top of the flexible ladder hooks over a windowsill. The rungs hang below. Escape ladders can be long enough to let people escape from several floors up. Experts recommend having an escape ladder in every upstairs room. The rungs fold up compactly to fit on a closet shelf. It's one of those gadgets that people hope they never have to use, but when it's needed, it could be a lifesaver.

SAFETY FIRST

WHEN FACING ANY FORCE OF NATURE,

it's important to know what to do before it happens, while it's happening, and after it happens. Wildfire is a powerful force of nature. Here are some ways to stay safe before, during, and after a wildfire.

Let's start with a couple basics that apply to any emergency situation.

BEFORE

PREPARE AN EMERGENCY KIT. Gather these items to keep in one place.

- Water: 1 gallon (3.8 L) per person per day for three days
- Food: enough nonperishable food to last three days
- Manual can opener for canned foods
- First aid kit
- Cell phone with charger
- Battery-powered radio and extra batteries
- Flashlight and extra batteries
- Whistle to signal for help
- Dust masks for each person
- Duct tape
- Local maps
- Wrench or pliers to turn off gas lines
- Moist towelettes and garbage bags for personal hygiene
- Change of clothing
- Items for infants, such as diapers and food
- Items for pets, such as pet food and extra water
- Extra cash and change
- Handkerchief to keep smoke out of your nose and mouth during a fire

PREPARE A FAMILY COMMUNICATION PLAN. Know how to get in touch with family members during an emergency, and practice your plan. Learn more on page 107.

Now here are some steps that apply specifically to fire.

CREATE A DEFENSIBLE SPACE. This space is a safety zone within at least 30 feet (9 m) of the building where fuels have been cleared, reduced, or modified. People can replace flammable trees and shrubs, such as pine, eucalyptus, and juniper, with less flammable trees, such as maple, oak, and other hardwoods. The cleared space also allows firefighters to work more effectively and safely.

KEEP AND LEARN HOW TO USE A FIRE EXTINGUISHER. Keep a fire extinguisher on each level of your home. Choose the A-B-C type so that you can use it on all types of fires, such as those caused by the burning of wood, gasoline, or electrical equipment.

INSTALL AND MAINTAIN SMOKE ALARMS. Have a smoke alarm on each level of your home. Test it and change the batteries at least twice a year.

KEEP A GARDEN HOSE HANDY. Make sure the hose is long enough to reach any area of the property.

PRACTICE WILDFIRE SAFETY. The Fire Smarts tips in this book are only a few ways to prevent wildfires. Check with your local fire department for others. Report dangerous conditions, like a downed power line. Plan escape routes away from your home.

USE PET STICKERS. You can get pet rescue fire safety stickers at a humane society or veterinary office. If you have a pet, put the sticker in the window to let firefighters know to look for the animal if a fire occurs while no one else is home.

DURING

IF YOU SEE A WILDFIRE but no firefighters, call 9-1-1. You may be the first one to report it. Then follow these steps.

EVACUATE IF AUTHORITIES ORDER OR ADVISE YOU TO DO SO. Take your emergency kit, wear long pants and a long-sleeved shirt, lock your home, and choose one of your escape routes. Tell someone when you left and where you are going.

PREPARE YOUR HOME, IF TIME. If you are not ordered to evacuate yet, help an adult prepare your home in case you do have to evacuate.

- Close all windows, vents, and inside doors to reduce drafts that could carry embers.
- Close garage doors.
- Have an adult shut off natural gas, propane, or fuel oil supplies.
- Place water sprinklers on the roof and leave them on for as long as possible.
- Move flammable furniture to the center of the room, away from windows.
- Lean a ladder against the house in plain view.
- Turn on a light in every room so the house will be visible through dense smoke.

IF CAUGHT OUTSIDE, LOOK FOR AN AREA WITH LITTLE OR NO FUEL. Don't try to outrun a wildfire. If a pond or river is nearby, go into the water and stay there until the fire passes. If a road is nearby, lie face down in the roadside ditch and cover yourself with anything that will shield you from the heat, such as wet clothing. If there is no road, go to any area with little or no vegetation, cover yourself, and lie face down. Breathe the air closest to the ground.

AFTER

THE FIRE MAY HAVE PASSED, but the danger hasn't. Take these steps to keep safe after the fire.

- Call 9-1-1 if you or others are injured.
- Go to a designated shelter if it is unsafe to return home after an evacuation. Don't enter your home until fire officials give the okay.
- Keep a lookout for flare-ups. After returning home, check the roof and attic for embers. Keep a lookout for any smoldering fires.
- Avoid downed power lines and poles.
- Keep an eye on pets. Don't allow them to roam loose. They might burn their paws if they wander into hot spots and embers. Pets also might be very nervous, so provide all the comfort you can.
- Throw away food that was exposed to heat or smoke.
- Be on guard for floods and mudflows. Rainwater often doesn't soak into charred soil, so it quickly runs over the land and down slopes. That could cause flash floods. The runoff carries ash and soil with it, creating mudflows. These risks may remain until vegetation grows back and stabilizes the slopes.

MY "SAFE" HOUSE GOES UP IN FLAMES

I FOLLOWED THE SMOKE PLUME

into the San Bernardino Mountains of Southern California. The hot and strong Santa Ana winds were pushing a fire into the mountain neighborhood of Smiley Park.

I drove until I came upon downed power lines that blocked the road. Fire had burned through the wooden pole, and the upper part had toppled over. Wires dangled and draped across the road like strands of spaghetti. I parked my car on the shoulder of the road facing away from the scene in case I needed to make a quick escape. I placed my keys on the dashboard. Both of these actions are standard procedures in wildfires. Then I took off on foot toward the black, billowing smoke.

All around me homes were in various stages of burning. I could barely believe what I was seeing. And at times, I could barely see. Thick smoke blew sideways and enveloped me like a black fog. I was so disoriented. I heard explosions and popping nearby in the smoke, but I couldn't tell what was happening. I knew one thing: Smiley Park had been evacuated. It was even too dangerous for firefighters, partly because of downed power lines and partly because fire engines wouldn't be able to turn around on the narrow roads. The neighborhood was a burning ghost town. So at least no one was in danger—except me.

I've been in situations in which I wonder if documenting a fire is worth the risk, and this was one of them. My head swiveled around, up and down, side to side. All my senses were on alert. I had never felt so confused, and I was concerned for my safety.

I felt better when I came upon a house that wasn't burning. I figured this could be my safe house. If the flames came too close, I could break the windows and

These photographs, taken a day later in the same spot in Smiley Park, California, show how completely this "safe house" was destroyed by the fire.

jump inside the house to ride out the fire. It would pass in 10 or 15 minutes. The sound would be terrifying, but the structure might protect me from the heat. That was my plan anyway. Turns out it was a lousy plan.

I walked around to take photos, but I always knew my way back to the house. I used an old, rusty pickup truck out front as a landmark. When I returned, however, my "safe" house was burning! Pine needles on the wooden deck had caught fire. The flames were small, but then I looked up. Black smoke was billowing out of the eaves around the house. This meant the attic was on fire. Soon the entire house would burn down.

I knew it was time to leave. Again I was disoriented. The noise of the wind and fire was deafening. The surroundings looked otherworldly. Banks of smoke had moved in and obscured trees and houses, even blocking out the sun. It took a few minutes to get my bearings. I had to navigate around many downed power lines, but I finally found my way back to my car and drove away.

NATURE'S SIGNAL

ONE OF THE STRANGEST THINGS I NOTICED THE DAY AFTER THE SMILEY PARK FIRE WAS THE TREES. Most of them still had their needles and leaves. That's evidence that the houses burned from embers flying from house to house, not from flames sweeping through the area.

The next day, I went back into the neighborhood. It was like I had never been there before. Everything looked so different. Then I saw the old pickup, and the thought hit me like a lightning bolt. "Hey, I'm in the same place." I was standing by the safe house of the night before. Except now there was no house. If I had stayed there, I might not have made it out.

FIRE RESEARCH

YOU KNOW YOU SHOULDN'T PLAY WITH FIRE, RIGHT?

A lot of fires start because people don't heed that advice. You might argue that some scientists "play with fire" for a living. Except, they aren't actually playing—they are doing important research.

Certain scientists work at fire research laboratories to learn more about fire. Through a variety of experiments, they help the public understand how fire starts, how it spreads, how best to fight it, and how to stay safe from it.

For example, in some experiments at the Missoula Fire Sciences Laboratory in Montana, scientists build a miniature forest made of shredded wood pieces hanging on rows of wire stands. The model forest is set on fire. Then scientists observe and measure how far apart the rows of trees have to be before the fire doesn't spread.

Other experiments involve setting a full-size house on fire. In a huge facility in South Carolina, U.S.A., researchers build a test house. Then they shower it with embers. The embers come from bark mulch that's set on fire. Fans blow the embers at the house through pipes. These experiments simulate the kind of ember storms that wildfires produce.

This research provides priceless information. Scientists learn more about how embers find their way into tiny openings and can ignite a structure. They test different kinds of roofing material, siding, gutters, windows, and vegetation to see which materials and designs resist fire. After the burn, the house frame can be fitted with other kinds of building

An "ember machine" at the Institute for Home and Business Safety (IHBS) in South Carolina, U.S.A., shows how quickly embers can light a house on fire.

FIREfact

DATA FROM SCIENTISTS' EXPERIMENTS are used to create computer models that help predict fire behavior. First, the perimeter of a fire is mapped. Then come data about the terrain, type of fuel, and weather. The model combines all these data and shows an animation of how the fire might spread. Different colors show areas that are most likely and least likely to burn. Maps from these animations are updated throughout the fire. The predictions provide a useful tool for firefighters on the ground. They also help managers decide how many people and pieces of equipment will be needed on certain fires.

materials for additional tests. The data from these tests lead to improved construction materials and safety tips for resisting fire damage.

Not all fire research is done in labs. Every few years researchers from Russia, Canada, and the United States get together and burn several hundred acres of timber to study crown fire behavior. Recently, these controlled burns have taken place in the Northwestern Territories of Canada. The scientists wait for weather that is cool and humid enough to conduct the tests safely. Then they use a flamethrower to set off the blaze. Besides studying how the fire behaves, researchers use the intense heat to test new materials for fire clothing, fire shelters, and roofs.

These are just a few ways that scientists conduct fire research. Their work is becoming more and more important as wildfires increase and more people move into the wildland urban interface.

A GROWING FIRE SEASON

The effects of drought are clear in this usually full reservoir in California.

TWENTY YEARS AGO, FIRE SEASON IN MOST PLACES RAN FROM LATE SPRING TO EARLY FALL.

In the Northern Hemisphere, this is roughly June through September. Times have changed. Now, fire season stretches from May to October, and in some places, it's even longer. Why has the fire season grown so much in a relatively short time? A major reason is the changing climate.

Climate change is making some places drier and hotter. California, for instance, has been setting records for the lowest amount of precipitation in the state's history. The rainy season starts later and ends earlier than it used to. Snowfall in the mountains has decreased, too. That means less water is available to fill reservoirs when the snow melts in spring. To make matters worse, higher temperatures draw moisture out of the soil and air. These dry, hot conditions make vegetation more vulnerable to fire throughout much of the year.

Today we live with a triple threat from wildfire.
1) Fuels have built up for a century.
2) More people are living in the wildland urban interface.
3) Climate change is making wildfires bigger, hotter, and more frequent.

This triple threat presents problems, but it also presents opportunities to find solutions. We know many of the solutions already, and people are acting on them. More and more people are accepting controlled burns as the best way to decrease wildfire fuels. In addition, people are learning about the ecological benefits of wildfire. They are adapting to wildfires by reducing risks.

Researchers, community leaders, and citizens will continue to work toward solutions to living with wildfire. And more than ever, the brave and tireless work of firefighters will continue to be one of the most important solutions to living with this extreme force of nature.

Ventura County / California

YARNELL HILL

FIGHTING WILDFIRES CAN BE EXTREMELY RISKY, ESPECIALLY IN THE WILDLAND URBAN INTERFACE. A GRIM REMINDER OF THIS OCCURRED IN THE SUMMER OF 2013 IN THE MOUNTAINS OF CENTRAL ARIZONA, U.S.A.

ON JUNE 28 of that year, lightning sparked a fire between the two old gold-mining towns of Yarnell and Peeple's Valley. The fire started out small, but dry winds whipped up the flames and pushed them straight for Peeple's Valley. Many of the residents were ordered to evacuate. Then on June 30, a sudden wind shift swung the fire around toward Yarnell. That town's residents also had to flee.

Many fire crews had been called in, including the Granite Mountain Hotshots from nearby Prescott, Arizona. This hotshot crew had just spent weeks battling two other fires, but they were used to the grueling conditions.

On June 30, the Granite Mountain Hotshots were digging line outside of Yarnell to protect homes. It's not known exactly what happened that day, but the changing winds and shifting flames certainly played a role. The hotshots became trapped. The lookout, who was stationed farther away, was rescued by another hotshot crew. They tried to rescue the rest of the Granite Mountain crew, but the heat was too intense. Tragically, the remaining 19 hotshots perished. It was the highest death toll of U.S. wildfire fighters in 80 years.

A memorial to the Granite Mountain Hotshots

The president of the United States said of the Granite Mountain Hotshots:

"THEY WERE HEROES—
HIGHLY SKILLED PROFESSIONALS WHO, LIKE SO MANY ACROSS OUR COUNTRY DO EVERY DAY, SELFLESSLY PUT THEMSELVES IN HARM'S WAY TO PROTECT THE LIVES AND PROPERTY OF FELLOW CITIZENS THEY WOULD NEVER MEET."

That statement sums up the way I, and so many others, feel about wildland firefighters and other first responders. They are all heroes.

HOW TO MAKE A FAMILY COMMUNICATION PLAN

ANY FIREFIGHTER WILL TELL YOU that communication is one of the keys to handling an emergency. You have to get good information and pass it along to others. So, one of the most important ways to stay safe in any emergency is to have a family communication plan. Here's what you do.

I. KNOW WHO TO CALL
Keep a list of people to contact in case you get separated during an emergency. Include parents, brothers and sisters, other relatives, neighbors, and friends. Fill out this list with a parent or other responsible adult. Be sure to include phone numbers for home, cell, and work.

2. KNOW THE WAY OUT
Make a map of your home showing all rooms, doors, and windows. Know two ways out of every room, if possible. Draw arrows on your map to show them.

3. KNOW WHERE TO MEET
Choose a special place outside your home where everyone in your family can meet up. It might be a tree or a light pole.

4. PRACTICE YOUR PLAN
Practice your plan twice a year, during the day and at night. Make sure the phone numbers on your list still work. Practice evacuating the house from different rooms and meeting at your special place.

No matter what the emergency, know how to keep in touch!

CONCLUSION

NO QUESTION, WILDFIRE IS EXTREME! I hope you have enjoyed learning about this powerful force of nature. I also hope you have enjoyed exploring the exciting world of wildland firefighters and discovering how these brave men and women protect us when wildfire becomes a threat.

Think about how this book has changed your ideas about wildfire and the people who fight them. Is there more to firefighting than you thought? What surprised you most?

Look back through the book. Pick out some favorite photos, and try to put into words what makes them special. What fire stories and other information stand out in your mind? Share interesting facts and ideas with others, just like I shared them with you.

You know that wildfires will become bigger, hotter, and more common in the years ahead. So you're likely to hear about them on news reports more often. When you do, think of the firefighters. Picture them sizing up the situation, hiking in, digging line, moving on, and digging more line. Feel the blistering heat from the summer sun as well as the roaring flames. Imagine the choking smoke, the eerie light, the rugged terrain.

Then think of the firefighters' outrageous skill, resourcefulness, and bravery. And when the news reports say the fire is over, you might just shake your head and say, "No, it isn't." You'll know the firefighters still face days or weeks of mop-up, when the work is just as exhausting, and often most dangerous.

So the next time you see any firefighters, thank them for their tireless work to keep you and the environment safe. I'll do the same.

RESOURCES & FURTHER READING

HERE ARE MORE WAYS TO EXPLORE THE WORLD OF WILDFIRE:

🔥 Check out more of Mark's favorite photos in this interview: kids.national geographic.com/explore/explorers/ meet-a-wildfire-photographer.

🔥 Here's a game you can play as you help a group of campers stay safe during a wildfire: ready.gov/kids/games/ data/dm-english/wildfire.html.

🔥 Put your knowledge to the test as you build an emergency kit during this game: ready.gov/kids/games/data/ bak-english/index.html.

🔥 Get your creative juices flowing as you view these colorful works of art from kids about wildfires and how to prevent them: firewise.org/wildfire-preparedness/teaching-tools/kids-corner/firewiseworksofart.aspx.

🔥 Keep track of current wildfires in the United States at this site: activefire maps.fs.fed.us/#.

🔥 Ride along with Mark through a wildfire in this video. You'll witness a fire tornado and see what it's like to have fields and forests going up in flames all around you: video.national geographic.com/video/mark-thiessen.

GLOSSARY

Adapt Change so as to live with new conditions

Arson The crime of purposely setting a fire to cause harm or damage

Backfire A fire purposely set to burn up fuel in the path of a wildfire

Black An area already burned and unlikely to burn further

Cold trailing One of the last stages of fighting a wildfire, in which firefighters carefully inspect the ground and feel for heat with their hands

Controlled burn A fire purposely set to clear out vegetation and help prevent a future, large wildfire

Crown The top, leafy part of a tree

Crown fire A devastating fire that jumps from treetop to treetop

Decomposition The breaking down of dead plants, animals, and other organisms

Descender A device used to descend, or climb down, a rope

Digging line Using tools to clear a path of any vegetation along the front of the fire

Drip torch A tool that drops small globs of flaming fuel on the ground to start a controlled burn

Drone A small, remotely controlled aircraft that can stay in the air for many hours at a time

Ecology The study of how living things interact with one another and their environment

Ecosystem All the living and nonliving things that interact in an environment, such as a forest or prairie

Ember A hot, glowing piece of wood or other fuel from a fire

Engine crew Firefighters who use vehicles, water, and fire retardant to fight wildfires

Evacuate Leave an area in an organized way for safety

Evaporate To turn from a liquid to a gas

Extinguish To put out a fire

Fertilizer Material that provides nutrients to help plants grow

Finger A narrow extension of fire from the main body of a fire

Fire camp An area set up as a headquarters for fighting a wildfire; also called base camp

Fire finder An instrument fire lookouts use to find the location of a wildfire

Fire line A narrow path cleared of vegetation that serves to stop an advancing fire; also called a firebreak

Fire retardant A chemical substance used to cool a fire or put it out

Fire shelter A foldable structure that helps protect a trapped firefighter

Fire triangle A model that shows how heat, fuel, and oxygen are needed to create fire

Fire whirl A spinning column of hot rising air that carries smoke and flame high up into the sky; also called a fire tornado

Flank A side of a wildfire; part of the fire's perimeter that is parallel to the direction the fire is moving

Friction The force of two surfaces rubbing against each other

Fuel Anything that burns

Fusee A small flare used to start a backfire or controlled burn

Germinate To sprout from a seed or other plant part

Green An area that has not burned but contains fuel, such as grass or wood

Habitat The place where a plant, animal, or other organism lives

Head The part of a wildfire that is spreading the fastest

Heel The part of a wildfire that is opposite the head and is usually spreading the slowest

Helitack The use of helicopters to attack a wildfire by transporting firefighters and equipment and dropping water or fire retardant onto the fire

Hotshot Highly trained wildland firefighter who uses hand tools to fight on the front lines of a wildfire

Humidity A measure of the amount of water vapor in the air

Ignite To begin to burn

Kindling Small pieces of fuel, such as grass, needles, and twigs, that burn easily

Ladder fuels Vegetation that provides a bridge, or ladder, between the ground and the upper parts of trees to allow flames to reach the tops of trees

Lookout A tower from which a wildfire can be seen and reported; the person who looks for fire from a lookout tower; a fire crewmember who observes a fire to warn others of danger

Mop-up The last major stage of fighting a wildfire, in which firefighters fell burned trees and check the ground for smoldering flames

Perimeter The edge of a wildfire

Personal protective equipment (PPE) Equipment and clothing carried and worn by a firefighter to provide safety and protection; includes fire-resistant clothing, hard hat, gloves, goggles, fire shelter, and other items

Pitch tube A small tube of a thick liquid that a pine tree pushes out of its bark to get rid of beetles that infest the tree

Point of origin The spot where a wildfire begins

Prescribed fire A controlled burn

Pulaski A tool for removing vegetation from the path of a wildfire; the head of a Pulaski has an ax on one side and a hoe on the other

Rappel A way of climbing down using rope attached to a point above

Resin A thick liquid produced by pine trees and other vegetation that is very flammable

Safety zone An area cleared of fuel and therefore safe for firefighters to go to during a wildfire

Sapling A small young tree

Smoke A mixture of gases, tiny liquid droplets, and fine solid particles called soot that don't burn up during a fire

Smoke jumper A wildland firefighter who reaches a fire by aircraft and parachute

Snag A dead tree; it can easily fall after a wildfire

Spot fire A fire caused from embers that blow away from the main fire

Terrain A specific kind of land, such as rocky, grassy, or wooded

Topography The shape of the land

Wildfire An uncontrolled fire in a forest, on a prairie, or in another type of wilderness area

Wildland firefighter A firefighter who fights wildfires

Wildland urban interface An area where development, such as homes and businesses, meets the natural ecosystem

INDEX

PHOTO CREDITS

If You Like
GOING TO EXTREMES ...

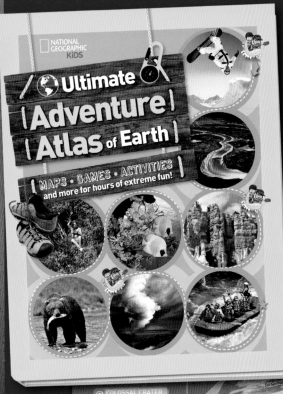

Take a flying leap into the planet's wildest places with this cool adventure atlas. Discover plants, animals, weather, and natural wonders. Enjoy hours of extreme fun with maps, games, and activities.

ON LOCATION

LAND OF FIRE AND ICE
Glaciers, volcanoes, and WATERFALLS

Slow-moving glaciers and fiery volcanoes have shaped southern Iceland. The Myrdalsjökull and Eyjafjallajökull ice caps both sit atop active volcanoes. When a volcano erupts, it punches through the ice in a cloud of steam and ash and lets loose a glacial flood. Because of the forces of fire and ice, the rugged landscape is dotted with lava fields, hot springs, craters, canyons, and waterfalls.

2 COLOSSAL CRATER
Eyjafjallajökull Glacier
Ride a jeep halfway up and then hike through the snow and ice to reach the one- to two-mile (1.6- to 3.2-km)-wide crater left by a 2010 volcanic eruption. Sky-high ash from the eruption halted air traffic in Europe for a week.

5 SCENIC TRAIL
Laugavegurinn
Trek through a landscape of deep canyons, glassy lakes, and steaming hot springs. Take in spectacular views of colorful mountains and rugged glaciers. Stop in a hut for the night. Look up and you may see the Northern Lights.

4 TURNED AROUND WATERFALL
Seljalandsfoss
Visit a sparkling waterfall where water cascades 203 feet (62 m) down the sheer cliff wall. Hike behind the falls and look through a wall of water. Don't forget your waterproof camera!

3 GREAT GLACIER
Sólheimajökull
Scale this icy giant to discover sparkling ice sculptures, rugged ridges, and deep crevasses. Try your skill at climbing an ice wall. Bring warm clothing, ice axes, and spiky crampons to slip over your boots.

DIGITAL TRAVELER!
There is a place in southern Iceland called Reynisfjara Beach. Search the Internet to find photos of its black sand and chunky rock columns. What colorful birds nest above the columns?

52

53

NATIONAL GEOGRAPHIC KIDS